John Reid

A Pocket System of Theology for Sabbath School Teachers

And Church Members Generally

John Reid

A Pocket System of Theology for Sabbath School Teachers
And Church Members Generally

ISBN/EAN: 9783337260552

Printed in Europe, USA, Canada, Australia, Japan

Cover: Foto ©Lupo / pixelio.de

More available books at **www.hansebooks.com**

A
Pocket System of Theology

FOR

Sabbath-School Teachers

AND

Church-Members Generally.

BY THE
Rev. JOHN REID,
AUTHOR OF "VOICES OF THE SOUL ANSWERED IN GOD," ETC.

WITH AN INTRODUCTION

By the Rev. JOHN HALL, D. D.

PHILADELPHIA:
PRESBYTERIAN BOARD OF PUBLICATION,
No. 1334 CHESTNUT STREET.

COPYRIGHT, 1884, BY
THE TRUSTEES OF THE
PRESBYTERIAN BOARD OF PUBLICATION.

ALL RIGHTS RESERVED.

WESTCOTT & THOMSON,
Stereotypers and Electrotypers, Philada.

INTRODUCTION.

There have been made in our time many and comparatively successful attempts to render into popular form and language the processes and results of those sciences which are commonly studied with care only by specialists. The effect has been good on the whole. The range of thought has been widened. The modest have been encouraged to prosecute study in departments which they would otherwise have deemed beyond their reach. Now, if men have thus gained on common lines of thought and investigation, surely yet more may be hoped from the like course in reference to theology—"the most excellent of the sciences."

The facilities—in the existing knowledge of religious truth and interest in it—are greater to the popular teacher of theology than to a like laborer in the fields of physical, or even of intellectual, science; and for this reason: that through God's goodness to the land there is wide acquaintance with the text-book, and there is a certain amount of exact knowledge in a multitude of minds. He who has, for example, committed to memory and retained there a good Catechism, has a certain preparation for further exact statement, and is prepared to appreciate truths in their relation to one another and to general thought and life.

Over against this must, indeed, be set the fact that the natural man is not in sympathy with spiritual things, and that human pride is all too ready to place revelation on the same basis with the results of human speculation. But on this very account it is all the more important to give definite information regarding the grounds of religious belief, and to show the elements that distinguish it from common conviction.

It is sometimes suggested in the press, and even in the pulpit, that the age does not want theology—that, in fact, it is an incumbrance to the Church. Humanity, culture, ethics (so called, as if theology did not carry with it the true and highest ethics!) and other vague terms are commended as describing the wants of the time. Of this two things may be said.

In the first place, whatever God revealed to man in ages past for his spiritual good must still be for that good unless some important element has undergone a radical change. But what radical change has taken place in the nature of God? or of man? or in their relations? or in the nature of moral evil? or of moral good? or of their influences on mankind?

And in the second place, it is generally conceded that in order to practical efficiency in the various departments of human effort exact intelligence must be kept within practical reach of the laborers. Discontinue the teaching of spelling and grammar, and the influence will soon appear in human speech and writing. Drop the study of mathematics, chemistry and allied sciences, and the influence will soon be felt in the related arts. So abandonment of exact theological teaching will soon be followed by loose thinking; but "as a man thinketh in his heart, so is he." Let sin, for example, be an unhappy incident, a slight misfortune, a piece of "bad form" simply, in a man's mind, and he will not be as watchful against it or as sorry for it as will one who has learned to count it transgression of God's law, of which the wages is death.

The author of this little book, deeply impressed with these convictions, aims at bringing theological inquiry to the level of ordinary intelligence. His previous efforts in the press entitle him, by their recognized character and influence, to speak again. He enjoys the confidence of his brethren. A venerable and trusted teacher of theology has read the work and given it approval, and from the examination I have been able to give to portions of it I do not hesitate to commend the work as fitted to guard against loose and inaccurate statement; to counteract the bad impressions made by indiscriminate sentences uttered in the interests of supposed " liberal" thought and specially broad charity; to show that the "dogmas" which are denounced are often not understood by their critics, and that the arbitrary decrees of Church authority in the Middle Ages are one thing, the doctrines given to men by inspiration of God are quite another.

JOHN HALL.

NEW YORK, 1st FEBRUARY, 1884.

PREFACE.

THE Puritans of the seventeenth century were theologians, and it was their theology which strengthened them and made them the great men of their age. When Holland, Scotland and New England lost their theology, they lost their power. The religion that despises doctrines is a religion that will be despised. A departure from orthodoxy, instead of being the sign of spiritual progress, is the sign of spiritual declension. It is morally impossible for saintly men like Leighton and Edwards to trample upon fundamental truth. The heart more generally leads to error than the head. The new is not always true, and the true is not always new.

There is needed just now a profound theological consciousness—that is, a sense of God, a feeling of awe and reverence, a high conception of the divine rectitude, in order to give tone to our views of the divine mercy—then a devotional spirit that will make the secular habit and the merely intellectual to be an impossibility. The end of all truth and life is worship—the rendering of glory to God. It was remarked of Dr. Bellamy that he made God to appear *great*. Modern preaching, teaching and training at home, will be more effectual if they possess that characteristic. Even the state papers of former times were noted for their theistic tone. (See those of Cromwell as instances.) The letters of Christian people also had a divine element running through them which we do not see to the same extent at present.

It has been said that every *science* has an *art* that is connected with it, as physiology has the art of medicine. So the science of theology runs into the art of religion, and gives practical effect to it. Religion is lifeless without theology, and theology is lifeless without religion. He who dislikes doctrine dislikes piety. Religion either ends in a dreamy sentimentalism or in a dry morality when it is divorced from the truth. The love of holiness and the love of doctrine must walk hand in hand together. Truth is light, and piety is the warmth which it brings. The *acts* of repentance and faith cannot be exercised unless first we have the *doctrines* of repentance and faith; just as we cannot have Christianity without Christ.

This small treatise on theology is not a skeleton. It is rather a body of divinity in *miniature*, having a full complement of bones and flesh and blood. Theological systems are large because the history of the doctrines is mixed up with them. Each topic by itself can be expressed in a few words. Often, the more one says the more confused the reader's mind becomes. The average intellect can grasp a thought best when it is presented in a few distinct sentences. Besides, the mass of Christians would not read through an intricate and voluminous system. The author, therefore, has been careful not to make his book long or difficult. One can carry it about with him and read a chapter when convenient, until the whole is finished. Having his mind awakened by the perusal, it is supposed that the reader will afterward seek for a more elaborate work.

Persons will differ in their opinion as to what should be left out and what retained in a book like the present. That it is more difficult to write a small volume on such a great subject than to write one that is larger, every thoughtful mind will admit.

Although the Bible is studied just now more than usual, it is a question whether the *doctrines* of Scripture are carefully pondered. Perhaps this manual may help Sabbath-school teachers and Christians generally in that direction. That a work of this kind is needed is the opinion of many learned men. Theology is so noble a subject that it would seem that every pious layman would be eager to look into it. Prof. Henry B. Smith makes the remark, " *that he who would spend his strength for that which is really influential, and always abiding in its influence, can best spend it in the service of Christian theology."*

Theology is not theory or speculation. It is founded on facts, truths, principles and persons, and these the most important in the whole realm of existence. Theology is pre-eminently the divine philosophy. It begins with God, comes forth to man, and shows how God and man may be united. Theology gives high meaning to time and eternity, to the course of nature and providence, to the fall of souls and their glorious redemption. The great problems of philosophy are equally the problems of theology, but with this difference: that theology is grounded upon a divine revelation, while philosophy works its way by principles of reason. The evangelical theology has such certitude, and meets man's needs so completely, that it must win the day.

CONTENTS.

PART I.

DOCTRINE CONCERNING GOD.

CHAPTER I.
Proofs of the Existence of God.................................. 13

CHAPTER II.
Attributes of God.. 21

CHAPTER III.
Triune God.. 29

CHAPTER IV.
Plan of God... 35

CHAPTER V.
God's Work of Creation.. 41

CHAPTER VI.

Providence of God.................................... 49

PART II.

DOCTRINE CONCERNING MAN.

CHAPTER I.
Origin and Antiquity of Man.......................... 58

CHAPTER II.
Innocence and Fall of Man............................ 67

CHAPTER III.
Sinfulness of Man.................................... 75

CHAPTER IV.
Free Agency of Man................................... 83

CHAPTER V.
Immortality of Man................................... 90

CHAPTER VI.
Man's Need of a Divine Helper........................ 96

PART III.

DOCTRINE CONCERNING THE PERSON AND WORK OF THE MEDIATOR.

CHAPTER I.

THE DIVINE-HUMAN MEDIATOR.................................... 103

CHAPTER II.

THE ATONEMENT OF THE MEDIATOR........................ 113

CHAPTER III.

CHRIST AS MEDIATOR BEFORE REDEMPTION—MEDIATOR DURING REDEMPTION—MEDIATOR AFTER REDEMPTION... 123

PART IV.

DOCTRINE CONCERNING THE PERSON AND WORK OF THE HOLY SPIRIT.

CHAPTER I.

THE HOLY SPIRIT.. 132

CHAPTER II.

ELECTION—THE PERSONS TO WHOM THE SPIRIT APPLIES THE DIVINE REMEDY... 140

CHAPTER III.

REGENERATION—DIVINE LIFE INTRODUCED INTO THE SOUL BY THE SPIRIT.. 149

CHAPTER IV.

Saving Faith—the Soul led to Rest on Christ by the Spirit 155

CHAPTER V.

Repentance—the Turning from Sin to Holiness by the Aid of the Spirit 163

CHAPTER VI.

Prayer—Holy Desire awakened by the Spirit ... 168

CHAPTER VII.

Sanctification—Progression in Holiness by the Spirit's Power till Perfection is reached 176

CHAPTER VIII.

Perseverance of the Saints—the Spirit never Leaves the Children of God 184

PART V.

DOCTRINE CONCERNING THE LAST THINGS.

CHAPTER I.

State of Souls between Death and the Resurrection 191

CHAPTER II.

The Millennium 198

CHAPTER III.
The Second Coming of Christ.................................. 206

CHAPTER IV.
The Resurrection of the Dead.................................. 212

CHAPTER V.
The Final Judgment... 218

CHAPTER VI.
The Future Punishment of the Wicked..................... 224

CHAPTER VII.
The Future Rewards of the Righteous..................... 234

Pocket System of Theology.

PART I.

DOCTRINE CONCERNING GOD.

CHAPTER I.

PROOFS OF THE EXISTENCE OF GOD.

THE soul has a native conviction that there is a God. This conviction is a necessity of the mind. All nations have an idea of a divinity. Even at the time when there is a belief in hundreds of gods, there is yet a belief in One who is above them all. Hence we read of "The First God," "The Great God," "The Supreme Governor and Lord of all," "The Self-subsisting Deity."[*] It does not follow from this that man has an intuition of God. It is more proper to say that he has a conviction of a supernatural Being, this conviction arising from a combination of powers, tendencies and needs in human nature, and from the world without as connected with the world within.

[*] Cudworth's *Intellectual System*, vol. i. p. 365.

To present proofs of the existence of God is an effort of reason; and, whether the proofs are sufficient or insufficient, God is still the same. Our logic neither makes nor unmakes him. To fair minds, however, a solid argument is a solid pleasure.

I. The Universe Points to a Creator.

There is a material universe; this universe is limited; being limited, it is not self-sufficient; it must therefore have come into existence. The Cause which brought it into existence must be outside of it; that Cause must have almighty power, as nothing less than almighty power could produce such an effect; that Cause must be mind, and that mind must be God.

If the matter is in a state of motion, the motion came from a Mover, and the Mover is God. If the matter acts according to specific laws, the laws point to a Lawgiver.

Is it said that there is no cause in nature, only antecedent and consequent? Be it so. The Cause is above nature, and that gives us the antecedent and consequent. There is assuredly an effect, and we know that every effect must have a cause. We are compelled, therefore, to believe in an extra-mundane God, the Creator of all things.

If we go back to the elements of matter, they can do nothing. The elements may have certain properties, but they never act unless they are brought in conjunction with other elements which match with them. The elements have no power to leap toward each other. They must remain stationary for ever unless there is a mind to use them for certain purposes. It is folly, therefore, to talk of the properties of matter as having power to form the universe. "Nothing which science has as yet established contravenes, invalidates, or hardly ever touches, the doctrine of creation—none of its evidence; the arguments for creation are just as strong and good as ever, and no established scientific principle or fact is in their way." *

Geology makes it certain that there was a long period in this world when nothing was in existence save inorganic matter; and yet when all was lifeless life came. From what did it come? Lifeless matter could not produce it. Life could come only from life. God must be the Giver of it. The first plant, animal and man were miracles of creation. All the kingdoms of life turn to God and bow to him. Science knows nothing of the origin of matter or of energy or of life. Admit the divine existence, and all is plain.

It is said, however, that God cannot be known; and yet the persons who say this speak of him as "The Infinite," "The Ultimate Cause," "The Creative Power." Certainly, if the Unknowable is *infinite*, is a *cause*, is *creative*, he *is known* to the extent of these characteristics. Since "we are obliged to regard every phenomenon as a manifes-

* Prof. H. B. Smith, *Lectures on Apologetics*, p. 186.

tation of some Power by which we are acted upon," * we *can know* something of the Power from its manifestation, just as we can know something of man from his works. The fact that I cannot comprehend the Infinite does not keep me from knowing many things about the Infinite. If there is no knowledge except the exhaustive, I am hopelessly shut out from it. Not even through eternity shall I be able to know God as he is, and yet all through eternity I shall know him more and more. God is concealed, yet revealed—unknown, yet known. If the human mind can make itself known, while the divine mind cannot, in that case the human excels the divine.

II. Design Points to a Designer.

The idea is self-evident that means arranged with reference to an end show intelligence. If blind forces have built the universe, why do they not build steamships and cathedrals? If they can do the greater they can do the less. The form, order and beauty that are manifest on every hand point to a Being who shapes and arranges, and who is himself the perfection of beauty. The sap that ascends the tree and the blood that flows through the system are manifestations of force, yet the force acts according to a plan. "*Order universally proves mind. The works of nature discover order. The works of nature prove mind.*" †

---

* Spencer, *First Principles*, p. 99. † Tulloch's *Theism*, p. 14.

The eye was made to see, the ear to hear, and the hand to grasp some object. When I behold men building bridges or composing treatises on atoms and necessity, I know they have a design in what they are doing. I must believe, then, that the intricate mechanism of the universe has a purpose which proclaims its Maker. "The invisible things of him from the creation of the world are clearly seen, being understood by the things that are made, even his eternal power and Godhead." Rom. i. 20.

See how light in passing through a prism branches off in different colors according to a fixed plan, giving us violet, indigo, blue, green, yellow, orange and red. Then how striking is the law that "every substance which emits at a given temperature certain kinds of light must possess the power at that same temperature of absorbing the same kinds of light"!* Design is seen in the elements as they mingle together in certain proportions; seen in the crystals which form the mountain of granite; seen in the ether which covers the immensity of space. All creatures upon earth are the expressions of certain types, giving us intimations of the skill of God. The two kinds of nerves, one conveying impressions to the brain, and the other motions from it, are notable instances of wisdom. The ants, with their industry, order, forethought and executive ability, seem

* Proctor, *The Sun Ruler of the Planetary System*, p. 119.

to be condensed minds, exhibiting more wisdom than the largest creatures. The fertilization of plants through the agency of insects, they carrying pollen from flower to flower, is a most wonderful adaptation of means to ends. The entire creation with its unity, giving us a *uni*-verse, points to the one God.

III. THE SOUL POINTS TO THE ABSOLUTE SPIRIT.

The material system cannot furnish the complete idea of God, because the material system is not a *person*. In man and nature we have the full proof.

I have an intellect: my Creator must be intellectual. That which has no understanding could not form a creature with understanding. I might as well say that the wind could originate life as to say that reasonless power could originate reason. Then I have feelings which excite and restrain, which love and hate: hence the Being that made me must feel. I can plan and purpose: God must have a will. "The personality of God is the ground of his relation with the personality of man. Without personality in God he would, so far as the knowledge of man goes, be lower than man, and without personality in man there would be no ground of relation to God."* To say that the Infinite cannot be a person is mere assertion.

* Mulford, *The Republic of God*, p. 26.

In the most exalted sense he is *the* Person. Then there is that which perplexes every materialist—consciousness: God must be a conscious Spirit. We have also the faculty of conscience. This does not merely show that the Divine Being has a moral nature. Guilt makes the soul to fear him as One who tries, condemns and punishes, thus giving us a divine Ruler and a divine government. There is no God but God, and conscience is his prophet.

The human spirit proclaims infinity and eternity: they must have an infinite and eternal ground; that infinite and eternal ground is God. When I look at great mountains and the starry heavens, I think of the Infinite. That men weary after they have obtained all earthly good is a cry for the Infinite. The finite does not match and measure the soul. Restlessness and despair are the midnight cry of man for God. There is a yearning for joys that never fail, showing that the mind was made for him. I am weak, helpless, dependent: I need the Independent. I have an idea of ultimate authority: I want the certain, the final—God.

If we turn from our nature to the man Christ Jesus, what a finished volume of evidence we find for God! How came this Sinless Soul to be here when the entire race to which he belongs is struck with evil? He is of us, and yet he is not of us. He is out of the range of our development. He had no prejudice, made no mistake, never fell short of his ideal, was the Man of men: how do we account for his appearance? Most assuredly, he is the image of God, proclaiming the divine existence with all the sacredness and certainty of eternal truth. He could say without the least misgiving, "He that hath seen me hath seen the Father." John xiv. 9.

The skeptic who has shaped the strongest argument to prove that there is no God has shaped the strongest argument to prove that there is one, because a mind that has such power is proof positive that there is a God. Sin is both theistic and antitheistic. Atheism never would have been thought of but for theism. "None deny there is a God," says Lord Bacon, "but those for whom it maketh that there were no God. It appeareth in nothing more, that atheism is rather in the lip than in the heart of man, than by this, that atheists will ever be talking of that their opinion, as if they fainted in it within themselves, and would be glad to be strengthened by the consent of others: nay, more, you shall have of them that will suffer for atheism, and not recant; whereas, if they did truly think that there were no such thing as God, why should they trouble themselves?" * Atheism is a kind of dead theism, because characteristics are ascribed to nature which belong to God. The sword of the atheist has two edges, but no handle. Every time

* *Essay on Atheism.*

he uses it he cuts himself. The greatest thought in existence is God, and the soul that has lost God is lost.

CHAPTER II.

THE ATTRIBUTES OF GOD.

The divine attributes belong to a nature, and that nature is pure spirit, this pure spirit having absolute simplicity, or oneness. There cannot be two Gods. One excludes a second. God is self-sufficient: his attributes are not conditioned by anything outside of him. He exists of necessity. The creation might sink into nothingness, and there would be no contradiction, but God must remain as he is. When we have a proper understanding of any single perfection of the Deity, we may logically infer other perfections from that, because there is nothing in him that is isolated.

1. The *eternity* of God. Eternity is stationary; time moves. God fills eternity, and lives in it. He has no past and no future—a constant present. If he lived moment by moment, as we do, he would be older at one time than at another. We cannot speak of God, however, as either old or young. He is the "I Am," the Being that Is, the King of the eternities. "From everlasting to everlasting thou art God." Ps. xc. 2. That which has no beginning

has no end. Beginningless existence is therefore divine and timeless. God is eternally conscious of all that is in his nature; he has therefore no reminiscence and no laws of association. He has no succession, because eternity is the mode of his existence; and yet, viewing him in relation to the universe, his acts appear to follow one after the other. He is thus unconditioned and self-conditioned. His eternity makes him timeless, while his perfection enables him to enter into time. Unless we are on our guard, we will make God powerless by very greatness—make him unable to do what man can do quite easily.

2. The *immutability* of God. If he were to change, he must change for the better or the worse. If for the better, he is imperfect; if for the worse, he is sinful; in either case he is not God. "I am the Lord, I change not." Mal. iii. 6. Infinite excellence conveys the idea that God has in himself every possible good. As the right and the true cannot change, so God being the source of these he cannot change. Unbounded space must remain as it is; so God being equally unbounded he must remain as he is. We can predicate change only of the finite. Independence and immutability are linked together. Immutability is not so much a single attribute as a characteristic of all the attributes. As the result of a purpose God may create, become incarnate, redeem, govern, without causing any change in the divine nature. It is not neces-

sary to be inactive in order to be immutable. The immutability of God is not to be viewed as a mere physical attribute, acting by a natural necessity. It has its true place when it is made to centre in the character of God. Immutability is then seen to be free absolute goodness. This destroys pantheism. If at one time God frowns upon a man, and at another time smiles upon him, this implies no change in the divine character, but it does imply that the man's character is changed from evil to good.

3. The *omnipresence* of God. Although God is a Spirit, and cannot be in space as matter is in it, he must be somewhere instead of nowhere. We conceive of our soul as in our body; so we say it is here, and not there: God being infinite, we speak of him as everywhere. "Do not I fill heaven and earth? saith the Lord." Jer. xxiii. 24. God is not only present where matter and mind exist, but is present beyond these. As he fills the eternal times without having to pass through years or ages, so he fills the infinite spaces without having to pass from one point to another. "The centre of God is everywhere; his circumference nowhere." While we believe in the divine immanence—that is, that God acts in nature—we equally believe that he manifests himself to the righteous as he does not to the wicked. The *remedial* influence which is brought to bear upon souls is different in *kind* from the power which sustains them.

4. The *omnipotence* of God. We know from

consciousness that power and causation are realities. If we have an infinite mind, we have infinite power. Omnipotence is sufficient for anything that does not imply a contradiction. Although the divine power is absolute, it must act in harmony with law, and not as blind force. Might does not make right. God can do many things that he never will do. The collective power of the creation is not the collective power of the Creator. Divine omnipotence and the divine will are not the same. The omnipotence of God is simple power: the will of God is power acting freely. Almightiness enters into every attribute, and in the order of nature it comes before the power which is moral. In the creation of matter and life omnipotence works without means: in certain other cases means are used. The creation of an atom is as truly an evidence of divine power as is the creation of a world. Almightiness arrests the attention of the race more quickly than any other attribute of the Deity.

5. The *omniscience* of God. The Divine Being sees everything at once by direct vision. He knows the nature of his own mind and all which it contains. A limitless spirit has limitless possibilities; consequently, God knows all that is *possible*. He knows also all that is *actual*, whether it relates to the past, present or future. This knowledge of the actual follows the divine plan: the knowledge of the possible precedes the divine plan. Another kind of knowledge has been imagined—

namely, the *conditionally possible*. For instance: a man dies at the age of forty. We say he might have lived till the age of sixty if he had been careful with his health. God knows how the millions of the saved would have sinned and suffered throughout eternity if they had been left to themselves. In these cases we see what *might have happened*. There is no need of this division of knowledge, as it comes under the classification of the possible.

6. The *wisdom* of God. "Wisdom is the excellency of knowledge." To be wise is a higher characteristic than to know. "Men may have knowledge without wisdom, but not wisdom without knowledge." Wisdom enables one to select the best end, and the best means of attaining that end. It is thus knowledge turned to good account. The divine wisdom is not a single attribute. It is a compound of knowledge, skill and goodness, and is both intellectual and moral. The only thing which clouds the wisdom of God to our mind is the fact of evil, and yet we must believe that that wisdom will appear all the more conspicuous as the divine system unfolds itself in the coming eternity. "Oh the depth of the riches both of the wisdom and knowledge of God! how unsearchable are his judgments, and his ways past finding out!" Rom. xi. 33.

7. The *self-determining power* of God. The divine will is preceptive when it commands and decretive when it purposes. The purpose of God to

glorify himself is called his antecedent will, and his purpose to create in order to manifest that glory is called his consequent will. If God is not absolutely free, he is held in the grasp of an absolute necessity. In that case he is not a person, but a characterless energy. The divine will, however, does not act independently of the nature which is back of it. God's will and God's reason blend together. The divine character is not found wholly in the divine will. God, by the perfections of his being, has moral excellence apart from the will, and, that moral excellence being complete, the will adopts it. The will cannot create righteousness. The righteousness has a nature of its own apart from the will. It is chosen because it is good—not merely good in the abstract, as if it were a power above God, but good as absolute worth in the very nature of God. This good because of its purity seeks the will, and the will because of its freedom seeks the good; and the union of the two gives us complete character. Mere will is reasonless, and mere nature is necessity; but a wise will blending with a loving necessity is the exalted liberty of God.

8. The *holiness* of God. Holiness is the inward purity of the divine character; or, in other words, it is "moral inviolability." The living creatures mentioned in the book of Revelation are represented as "resting not day nor night, saying, Holy, holy, holy, Lord God Almighty!" Rev. iv. 8.

This utterance of the word "holy" three times conveys the idea of great sacredness. The Divine Being shrinks from the least taint of evil, but finds infinite delight in goodness. God may create a universe or not as he pleases, but he cannot love holiness or not as he pleases. As "it is impossible for him to lie," it is impossible for him to make choice of sin.

9. The *justice* of God. Justice is that moral quality which leads God to give all creatures their due. "Shall not the Judge of all the earth do right?" Gen. xviii. 25. When fallen man is left with the simple theology of conscience, and is not quieted by false arguments, his eye centres more on God's justice than on God's mercy. Justice is ultimate, and is therefore more comprehensive than mercy. The greatest good of the greatest number, or the greatest happiness of the greatest number, is not the reason why God acts justly. He acts justly because it is right to do so. The justice of God is seen in his works and words, in his deeds and revelations, in his guidance and government, in his decisions and punishments. God may be just, and yet give the righteous a greater reward than they deserve; but he cannot be just if he inflicts upon the wicked a greater punishment than they deserve. If God makes a gracious promise, justice compels him to fulfill it.

10. The *love* of God. God loves his own being and character, and finds complete satisfaction in

himself. Not only does love furnish a principle of unity to the creation, but it furnishes a principle of unity to the Creator. There is with God the *love of benevolence.* This is good-will; it seeks the well-being of the creature. God has not originated any contrivance for the mere purpose of producing pain. The normal working of all creatures ends in happiness. Infringement of law ends in pain. God being *the* good, he has no motive which prompts to evil. There is also the *love of complacency.* This is delight in goodness and delight in worth of any kind. God never can look upon the wicked and the righteous in the same way. He must hate sin and love holiness. It was benevolence which led God to provide a way of salvation for lost men; and when men were restored to the divine image it was complacency which led God to find delight in the change. Pity goes out to those in distress; forbearance arises in view of the perversity of men; mercy has special reference to the guilty.

11. The *truth* of God. God is truth, even as he is love. Whatever his declarations may be, they must be true. The promises of God are sometimes absolute and sometimes conditional. They are absolute, as in the promise of redemption through Christ, and in the promise of seed-time and harvest while the earth remains. They are conditional, as when forgiveness follows repentance, and salvation follows faith. God is truthful in his offers

of mercy to men, although he knows that many will reject these offers. A father may desire the reformation of his son when it is certain that the son is fixed in his evil habits. Divine punishment will assuredly be meted out to the wicked.

Blessedness connects itself with the entire working of the divine nature. The fact that the attributes of God are in a state of harmony shows that he must be for ever blessed. There being no deficiencies in the Infinite Mind, there is nothing but infinite enjoyment.

CHAPTER III.

THE TRIUNE GOD.

NEITHER angel nor man knows of himself whether God should exist as one person or as three persons. The subject is beyond the reach of the finite understanding. The universe points to one God, but as to whether this one God has a plurality of distinctions or not the universe is silent.

I. A DIVINE TRINITY NOT IMPOSSIBLE.

We know that a human soul and a human body can be so united as to make one man. This is wonderful, and the wonder is heightened from the fact that the soul and the body are different substances.

If two unlike substances can thus constitute one man, is it unreasonable that two persons having the same substance should constitute one God? Again: if we have an *I*, does not that make necessary the existence of a *Thou?* Is it to be supposed that a Being like God dwelt in absolute solitude throughout a past eternity? Are not an I and a Thou necessary in the very constitution of the Deity, and equally necessary to furnish communion during a dateless existence? This at least is possible. Besides, does not *love*, from its nature, demand an *object*, and divine love a divine object? It would seem so. In this way we have a plurality of persons in the Godhead, and the sweetest fellowship as a result of it.

But do not love and its object, the I and Thou, the body and soul, suggest simply two persons? That is all. It may be, however, that it is easier to conceive of three persons in the Godhead than two. Two persons seem to stand apart like two pillars, there being nothing to connect the one with the other. In the case of the soul and the body there must be a *something* which unites the two together, thus presenting a certain kind of threefoldness in the constitution of man. In the same way the divine I and Thou, the divine love and its object, must have a divine bond of union; and this bond of union gives us the third person of the Godhead.

It would seem also that a voluntary mind can

come only to full self-consciousness by a threefold movement. 1. There is the mind as subject. 2. There is that mind viewing itself as object. 3. There is the same mind resolving itself back into unity. Now, in the Godhead the Father may be thought of as the eternal subject; the Son, as the eternal object, expressing the divine fullness; and the Spirit, as that person who eternally resolves the subject and object back into unity.

These thoughts are not presented as proofs of the Trinity; they simply show that it is not an impossible doctrine. Let them be accepted, then, for what they are worth.

II. Evidence of the Divine Trinity.

The Bible is the only source of proof. Let us begin with this passage: "Go ye therefore, and teach all nations, baptizing them in the name of the Father, and of the Son, and of the Holy Ghost." Matt. xxviii. 19. Three persons are spoken of here, and the three are put upon a level. Those who are baptized are baptized in the name of the three persons. Baptism is an act of worship, and the worship is made to centre in the three persons. How could this be if they were not divine? Suppose the formula were to read in this way: Baptizing them in the name of God the Father, and of the created Son, and of the Holy Spirit as divine influence,—would not the whole be without meaning? As the passage stands it is a sublime declaration respecting the three persons of the Godhead: when a man is baptized he feels that he is set apart to the service of the Triune Deity. "Baptism has always been administered in the Church in the name of the Father, the Son and the Holy Ghost. How ineradically this usage was fixed in the Church appears most clearly from the fact that even those to whom the formula was dogmatically unsuitable—the Ebionites, for instance—did not venture to dispense with it."*

Take, now, the apostolic benediction as further evidence: "The grace of the Lord Jesus Christ, and the love of God, and the communion of the Holy Ghost, be with you all. Amen." 2 Cor. xiii. 14. Here again is an act of worship, and the same three persons are mentioned as in the formula of baptism. *Grace* as centring in Christ, *love* as centring in God, and *communion* as centring in the Holy Ghost, express personality; and that the three persons are equally divine is the fair inference from the passage. Christ is even placed *first* in the benediction—a strange thing if he is not one of the persons of the Godhead.

Observe this other passage: "Elect according to the foreknowledge of God the Father, through sanctification of the Spirit, unto obedience and sprinkling of the blood of Jesus Christ: grace unto you, and peace, be multiplied." 1 Pet. i. 2.

* Dorner, *Doct. of the Person of Christ*, vol. i. p. 168.

Here is the same threefold arrangement. The salvation of the Christian is not traced back to one divine person: all the three bear a part in this great work.

III. Explanation of the Divine Trinity.

The doctrine is partly mysterious and partly plain. The mysterious part is above the reason, but not contrary to it. The use of the word "person" demands notice. A person, in common language, has a distinct nature of his own. Not in this way are we to understand the different persons of the Godhead, because if each person had a distinct nature we should have three Gods. The meaning of the word "person," therefore, is peculiar. There is but *one divine nature* to all the three persons. In this way we have a trinity in unity. God is not one in the sense in which he is three. I could not say that three men are one man, for they have three distinct natures, but I can say that three persons are one God, for they have only one divine nature.

The question may be asked, Are there three sets of divine attributes? No: that would give us three Gods. There is but one omnipotence, one omniscience; and so with all the other attributes. Each person may be spoken of as infinite, because the one infinite essence belongs to all the three in common. There are not three infinities in the sense of three infinite natures, as that would be tritheism.

We reach now the point that the Trinity is found in the very constitution of the Godhead. It is not dependent on anything out of God for its existence, neither is it any threefold method of divine manifestation. As far as our knowledge of the Trinity is concerned, that knowledge comes to us in connection with the plan of redemption; but even if there were no redemption, the Trinity would still be a fact of the Godhead.

There is an order among the divine persons. The Father comes first, the Son second, the Spirit third. It is not to be understood, however, that there are degrees of greatness among the persons. They are all equally divine and equally eternal. It was the place of the Father to send the Son, the place of the Son to assume human nature, and the place of the Spirit to purify the soul. There is a something which characterizes the Son that does not characterize the Father, and a something which characterizes the Spirit that does not characterize the Father and the Son. There is a property which marks off each person, and that property is incommunicable. "The Son is never said to send the Father nor to operate through him; nor is the Spirit ever said to send the Father or the Son, or to operate through them."* If the three persons were alike in every respect, their identity would be lost: they would be resolved into one person. The Father is not God independently of the Son, nor the Son God

---

* Dr. Charles Hodge, *Systematic Theology*, vol. i. p. 445.

independently of the Father, nor the Spirit God independently of the Father and the Son: the three persons constitute the one God.

The Trinity is not merely a speculative doctrine, as some scholars would have us believe; it is intensely practical. It forms the basis of the whole redemptive process and fits the wants of the sinful mind. I am estranged from God; I want a Mediator; I want a Sanctifier: thus man's need points to the three divine persons.

CHAPTER IV.

THE PLAN OF GOD IN GENERAL.

THE plan of God presupposes that he has an ultimate end which governs him. What is that ultimate end? It is self-manifestation. When we say that God makes *himself* his chief end, his *glory* his chief end, and the *manifestation* of his glory his chief end, the meaning is essentially the same in each statement. There is no selfishness in this, because "God is love." He being the *highest good*, the design is to manifest that good throughout infinite space and endless time. The *entire excellency* of the divine nature and character is called "the *glory* of God."

Let us go back in imagination to the time when nothing existed save the Divine Being. Why should he create? No reason can be found outside of God, because nothing exists. He is thus thrown back upon himself to find in himself his chief end. If God was his own end before the creation, he must continue for ever to be his own end: the creation cannot furnish a motive that is greater than the Creator. In this idea of divine manifestation we can see that God is unwilling to remain by himself. So glorious and blessed is his nature he would diffuse himself in radiant forms through eternity and immensity. We behold nothing in the universe, evil excepted, but streams from the infinite Source of life. Though the essential glory of God receives no increase, his manifested glory spreads out with augmenting power for ever; and as his eye penetrates the vast deep of an endless futurity, beholding the mighty succession of spirits and men, and these drawing nearer and nearer to him, he sees his own ultimate end ever shining forth above all, while the creatures of his power are made joyful in the one chief purpose and in the one increasing manifestation. The glory of God and the good of the universe are linked together. "Thou art worthy, O Lord, to receive glory and honor and power: for thou hast created all things, and for thy pleasure they are and were created." Rev. iv. 11.

That God has a *plan* is an idea that commends itself to the human reason. It can be illustrated in the following way: I intend to build a house. The style of architecture, size of the edifice, number of the rooms, doors and windows, and many other things, are all sketched out, and the building is to be erected according to the plan. Even the persons who shall work on the building and the wages they shall receive are determined upon. Nothing is left to chance. So God makes selection of a plan for the universe. We should have no evidence of the divine existence if all were confusion. The creation reveals laws that are certain, showing that all is fixed. The fact that God has originated matter and mind leads us to say that he always intended to originate them. Thus we are led back to an eternal plan. The divine acts are simply the outworking of the divine purpose. As the painting of the artist points back to an ideal he had in his mind, so the marvelous painting of the creation points back to the ideal which God had in his mind. "The Lord of hosts hath sworn, saying, Surely as I have thought, so shall it come to pass: and as I have purposed, so shall it stand" (Isa. xiv. 24); "I am God, and there is none like me, declaring the end from the beginning, and from ancient times the things that are not yet done, saying, My counsel shall stand, and I will do all my pleasure." Isa. xlvi. 9, 10.

Does the foreknowledge of God precede his decree? or does the decree of God precede his foreknowledge? The Arminian theologians believe that foreknowledge comes first. Omniscience, they say, is an attribute, and so it must be viewed as existing before an act of the divine will. We admit that God knows all that is *possible* previous to any decree. Out of an infinite number of possible systems, however, God selected one. That one system was then known as the *actual* system, and not as the possible. The choice of the system, therefore, must, in the order of thought, precede the knowledge of that choice. If I think about building a ship, I cannot tell what kind of a ship I shall build until I have made choice of a plan. I may know of hundreds of possible plans, all suitable for different kinds of ships, but not till I *select one particular plan* can I know of the ship I am to build. Of course, in the mind of God his decree and foreknowledge are equally eternal, yet according to a principle of order the decree precedes the foreknowledge. This is the way the Calvinistic theologians view the matter.

"Foreknowledge," we are told, "does not make events certain—it only *proves* them so." This is correct. The events, however, must be made certain in some way; and in what way can that be but by the divine purpose? If neither the divine foreknowledge nor the divine purpose makes events certain, we are thrown into complete confusion. Foreknowledge, however, really necessitates foreordination. "If God foreseeing that if he created a certain free agent and placed him in certain relations, he would freely act in a certain way, and yet with that knowledge proceeded to create that very free agent and put him in precisely those positions,

God would, in so doing, obviously predetermine the certain futurition of the acts foreseen." *

There is an idea floating in many minds that if God decrees that a thing shall be, he *makes it to be* by his own efficiency, and thus destroys human freedom. Certainly, in the case of sin he *does not* make it to be, although by a definite purpose he *permits* it to be; and when he decrees that men shall be wise and good he works through the medium of their thoughts, feelings and actions. It is just as impossible to take freedom from the mind as it is to bestow freedom upon matter. A general may lay out the plan of a great campaign, making it certain that thousands of men will act in thousands of ways as the result of that plan, and yet the liberty of no one be infringed upon. The father of a family can make numbers of things certain among his children by reason of a governing purpose, they meanwhile being perfectly free in all their movements. All of us are foreordaining what comes to pass in certain spheres, with no loss of liberty in those who are affected by us. If a man can thus act, surely a Being of infinite resources can arrange all the affairs of his empire without encroaching upon human freedom. If God has no such sovereignty in his dominions, then he is merely a spectator, watching to see what his creatures will do, dependent upon them, and not they upon him.

* A. A. Hodge, *Outlines of Theology*, p. 203.

The divine decree touching sin is that which perplexes certain minds. Now, that God has chosen a system with sin in it is a fact. We therefore have these different links in the chain: 1. It is certain that *all men sin.* 2. It is certain that God *permits* all men to sin. 3. It is certain that he *chose* to permit them to sin. 4. It is certain that he *foreknew* they would sin. If a man selects a site for a house which, with many advantages, has the one disadvantage that a miasmatic taint is found there, it will be hard to prove that the miasmatic taint did not enter into the man's calculations. Of course it was not for the sake of the evil that the man made choice of the place, and yet he did make choice of it knowing that the evil was there; so that, in a sense, it had some relation to his will: he chose to have the evil rather than not have the particular site for his house. He never approved the evil, but always condemned it, and put himself to great trouble and expense in order to destroy it; being conscious, however, that it never would be completely overcome. Just why he chose that one spot for a house, when there was certain danger connected with it, has never been known. Whether he meant that the evil should be a warning to others, or whether the advantages of the place were of such a high order that it was better to have them with the evil than to have lesser advantages without it, we cannot say. One thing is clear: the man did not originate the miasmatic taint. It was at the most only negatively adopted, the affirmative choice resting supremely on the fine advantages of the place. All we can say is, that it was brought into the purchase of the site by a permissive decree. So the Most High purposed to permit sin, using no efficiency to produce it.

CHAPTER V.

GOD'S WORK OF CREATION.

IN the first chapter of Genesis we have the chief account of the creation. There we learn that the heavens and the earth had a beginning. The Hebrew word *bara*, which is translated by the word *created*, means " to cut, to cut out, to form by cutting and carving." Certain persons have therefore thought that it cannot be used in the sense of creating out of nothing. It is the best word, however, which the Hebrew writer could use to express absolute creation. If we must in all cases follow the primary sense of words, we shall be nothing but materialists. When we speak of the spiritual and the unseen, we have to put a meaning into language that thus it may express spiritual and unseen realities. We cling, then, to the great truth, "that things which are seen were not made of things which do appear." Heb. xi. 3. A creation destroys atheism, and a Creator destroys pantheism. The one overshadowing thought in the first chapter of Genesis is the *personality of God*. That first chapter is so dense with meaning, so orderly and sublime, so pure and impressive, that divinity radiates from every part of it.

With regard to a correct interpretation of this opening portion of the Bible, it is a question whether any one can furnish it at present. Certain writers suppose that all the changes of the ancient earth took place during that vast period which intervened between the creation of matter and the advent of the first day, and that after the long ages of geology had ended, then began the work of the six literal days of creation—a creation that is modern. Others think that the days of Genesis represent great periods. We adopt this latter view.

The word "day" has different meanings. In Gen. i. 5 it is used to mark the time of *light* as contrasted with the darkness: "God called the light day." Both evening and morning are also called day, while in Gen. ii. 4 it is made to cover the whole work of creation: "These are the generations of the heavens and the earth when they were created, in the day that the Lord God made the earth and the heavens." We speak of "the day of salvation," showing that the word has an extended meaning.

Objection is made to this use of the word "day," on the ground that it seems to clash with the fourth commandment, where the language is: "In six days the Lord made heaven and earth, the sea, and all that in them is, and rested the seventh day: wherefore the Lord blessed the sabbath day, and hallowed it." Ex. xx. 11. The real thought may be that God had a working week suited to his nature, a week measuring vast cycles of time. During the continuance of this great week of the Almighty he was at work. Having labored for six long periods till the earth and the heavens were finished, he then rested during a seventh period. This seventh period is manifestly not of twenty-four hours, because it still continues. And, what is worthy of special attention, there is no mention of an evening and a morning on that seventh day of God's rest. This may intimate that the divine sabbath is of long continuance—that it is to extend over all the centuries of human time, and thus be the great redemptive day to bless fallen men. As God rests during the seventh day of his week, what more fit than that man should rest during the seventh day of his week, that thus he may keep in remembrance the work and ways of the Most High? The Sabbath of man is in proportion to his week, and the Sabbath of God is in proportion to his; so there is no contradiction.

That the earth with its plants and animals existed long before the time of Adam is evident. There are rocks which were formed by gradual additions of matter. Sediment was collected year after year and age after age, and thus those rocks increased in size. As the rivers swept along their course, particles of matter mingled with the waters and settled at the bottom or were carried to the mouth of the stream and formed there tracts of land. Thus we have sedimentary rocks, and deltas like those of the Rhine and the Mississippi. Remains of animals are found imbedded in the rocks, which prove that the earth is of great antiquity.

What the original state of matter was neither the Bible nor science informs us. Our globe at one time may have been a fiery ball in space. Then by degrees the surface may have cooled, leaving the centre a mass of fire. Volcanic eruptions seem to sustain such a view. The condition of the earth as first mentioned in Genesis must have been long after that fiery period, because the waters then covered it. To say that the waters refer to matter in its gaseous state seems like forcing language into harmony with a theory.

In looking over the narrative of the creation one or two striking facts arrest the attention. For instance, there is the appearance of the vegetable kingdom before the animal. This is the logical order, the lower coming into existence before the higher. It is also the chronological order—the creating of food, then the creatures that were to use it. "Science gathers but indistinct records from the earth on this point, yet plainly has no counter-statement; and as far as there are any indications, they favor the above." Vegetation was also necessary in the plan of God for the formation of coal; thus there was a preparation through untold ages for the comfort and advancement of man.

Another point, noticed by Professor Guyot, is the *double work* which takes place on the *third* day and also on the *sixth*. The dry land was made to appear and the plant kingdom introduced—both on the third day. The organic period must begin before the inorganic period ends. The double work on the sixth day is the creation of mammals and man. Here, while the whole comes to a climax, the climax has a finger pointing ahead. Though man is the last link in the chain, he is at the same time the beginning of a new order of things. Moral law is now seen to take the place of physical law, and he who is made in the image of God is to be the subject of the divine administration, having a life and a character that are to continue for ever.

"The *Bible* says that MAN was the last creation. *Geology* says the same.

"The *Bible* says that quadrupeds next preceded man. *Geology* says the same.

"The *Bible* says that inferior animal species, up to reptiles, were created before quadrupeds. *Geology* says the same.

"The *Bible* says that there was, earlier, an age without animal life. *Geology* says the same.

"The Bible says that after the world had been

long in formation (for its three days) the sun, moon and stars appeared in the heavens. Geology also makes this an event long after the earth's beginning.

"Thus it is clear that there is an accordance to a considerable extent, and that facts in science are stated in the Bible, although not there recorded simply as scientific facts." *

The existence of a class of beings higher than man may now be noted. It is reasonable that an order of intelligences should fill the space between man and God. The Bible makes mention of angels, but does not say when they were created. It is evident, however, that they were called into being before the time of Adam. They are not a race, but were created as distinct persons, and evidently at one time. Angels are *spirits*, and Christ informs us that "a spirit hath not flesh and bones." Thus they are immaterial. The language, "angel of light," does not point to any physical organism: it rather marks the contrast between the good and evil angels. It is true that the angels who appeared to Abraham looked like men, and equally true that those who were seen at the sepulchre of Christ had the human form; but we cannot reason from such facts that they are corporeal beings. The likelihood is, that the body was only assumed for a special occasion, just as one of the persons of the Godhead took the human form in Old-Testament times when

* Prof. Dana, in *Biblioth. Sacra*, vol. xiv. p. 520.

he appeared to men. Theophanies and angelophanies are of the same character—transient appearances. The fact that angels are invisible to us at present would intimate that they are immaterial. If the possession of a body were natural to them, it could be seen now as well as formerly. The idea that no finite intelligence can act without a body is merely a speculation. Reason is not able to make that point certain.

Angels are spoken of as "innumerable;" their power is seemingly miraculous; Peter was delivered out of prison by an angel. They take part in the chief transactions of this earth, and manifest great interest in the plan of redemption. They were present at the giving of the Law; they proclaimed peace to the nations when Christ came; they ministered to the Saviour during the days of his humiliation; they rejoice when men turn to God; they comfort and support the righteous amid the trials and temptations of life; they convey them to their eternal home at death; they will bear a part in the solemn scenes of the final judgment. In fact, they are a kind of celestial missionaries laboring with intense love for the salvation of men—a love that is all the greater in that no man beholds it, and in that they receive no thanks from men. These noble spirits are of different orders, as principalities and powers, thrones and dominions. Gabriel seems to be sent on special embassies, and Michael is officially marked off as the archangel.

Respecting the fallen angels a few thoughts may be stated. They must have sinned shortly after their creation, because if they had lived for years in a state of purity a habit of holiness would have held them fast. Their first sin has been thought to be pride, from this passage: "Not a novice, lest being lifted up with pride he fall into the condemnation of the devil." 1 Tim. iii. 6. Another view is that the first sin of the angels consisted in their unwillingness to render due homage to the Son of God. The passage which suggests this is in these words: "When he bringeth in the first-begotten into the world, he saith, And let all the angels of God worship him." Heb. i. 6. Still another opinion, expressed by an eminent writer, takes this form: "Whilst Lucifer was a good angel he saw *in the very countenance* of God that he had from eternity resolved to become a man in time, and to assume, not the nature of angels, but the nature of men; and this stirred up his *envy* and caused his fall." *

Persons object to the idea of fallen angels, supposing that beings with such comprehensive knowledge never would have allowed themselves to sin. This proves nothing, for we see men of the highest attainments utterly godless. Others say that it is contrary to the benevolence of God for him to permit angels to tempt men to sin; consequently, there are no such beings. It is certain that God

* Dorner, *Doct. of the Person of Christ*, Divis. ii. vol. ii. p. 77.

permits men to tempt each other and to ruin each
other. The objection, therefore, has no value. The
personality of Satan and of the unclean spirits is
denied, individuals understanding the language to
represent bad feelings and principles, not bad angels. Christ declares that the world of woe was
" prepared for the devil and his angels " (Matt. xxv.
41), and Jude speaks of "the angels who kept not
their first estate," telling us that "God hath reserved them in everlasting chains under darkness
unto the judgment of the great day." Principles
are not punished, but persons. Satan is called "the
prince of the power of the air " (Eph. ii. 2), as if he
were the ruler of the hosts of darkness. He may
have been the first that sinned, and the first that
led the other angels into evil. The fallen powers
must be numerous, because their malign influence
reaches all mankind. The plural "devils," which
we find in different parts of the Bible, should be
demons. There is only one devil, but many demons. He who resists these foul spirits will be
stronger for ever; he who yields to their influence
will be doomed for ever.

CHAPTER VI.

THE PROVIDENCE OF GOD.

ALL systems admit a *something* that is beyond
nature, and works through it. This something
may be viewed as Fate, or as Force, or as the

Nameless Infinite, or as God. No man rests in what he sees. Divine providence is a necessity of ultimate truth and ultimate thought, and a necessity of the feelings of weakness, awe and fear. The "Positive Philosophy" is philosophy without the positive Being. It is the playing with laws after having rejected the Lawgiver—playing with second causes after having rejected the First Cause. There is no evidence that a single one of the fallen angels is an atheist. Atheism is a sin peculiar to men.

" By "divine providence" is meant the preservation and government of the universe. Our word " providence " is from the Latin *providentia*, and means foreseeing, forethought, timely care and prudence. A teacher exercises providential care over a school, a merchant over his business, a father over his family, and a monarch over his subjects. That providence is not a fancy is evident from the fact that the human race generally believe in it. The Bible makes it certain: " He giveth to the beast his food, and to the young ravens which cry " (Ps. cxlvii. 9); "Lord, thou wilt ordain peace for us: for thou also hast wrought all our works in us" (Isa. xxvi. 12); "All my springs are in thee" (Ps. lxxxvii. 7); " For of him, and through him, and to him are all things : to whom be glory for ever." Rom. xi. 36.

The *method* of providence is more perplexing to us than the *fact*.

One theory affirms that God *acts directly* upon all created things. Nature, as such, is destitute of power. It can neither begin nor continue without the divine agency. Absolute dependence is the characteristic of the entire creation. Laws of nature are simply names for the uniformity of the divine action. The power of God, directed by wisdom and goodness, explains all the changes of the universe. "In him we live, and move, and have our being." Acts xvii. 28. This view is adopted by many distinguished scholars.

Another theory believes that God acts through *second causes*. These second causes are viewed as facts in nature, and also as the workmanship of God. It cannot be denied that the elements act when they are brought together in certain relations. Let the heat of the sun reach water, and vapor ascends. Let the air be cooled, and the vapor is changed to rain. Let the moon's influence reach the ocean, and we have the tides. When steam is generated it becomes a power to drive machinery. The air is a force, and is the medium by which sound travels. Electricity conveys the commerce of the mind. These second causes, however, need the guidance of an intelligent being. Steam and electricity will accomplish little unless man directs them. In the same way God uses second causes to carry forward his designs. The elements of nature are his agents. "Fire and hail, snow and vapor, stormy wind, fulfill his word." Ps. cxlviii.

8. This view strikes us more favorably than the other.

To say that the providence of God is general is not sufficient: it is universal, and in that way it is particular. A sparrow cannot fall to the ground without his permission, and the hairs of our head are all numbered. A *special* providence is from its nature limited. The Israelites crossing the Red Sea in safety, the fatal wounding of Ahab from a bow drawn at a venture, and the conversion of Paul, were special providences. When the French fleet of forty ships, coming against New England in 1746, was destroyed, that was a noted instance of a special providence. Miracles are special providences. God may use second causes or he may not in working miracles: in either case there is divine intervention. Miracles are not the result of some higher law in nature, as if a clock were made to strike a *hundred times* at the end of a hundred years, while before the end of that period it struck the hours as usual. A miracle is supernatural, but not a violation of the laws of nature. All the dead might be raised in a moment and no jar be given to the universe. No consistent theist can object to miracles. Only in the systems of atheism and pantheism are they out of place.

"The believer in Christ's miracles," says Professor Calderwood, "may fairly ask of scientific critics that they state any law of nature which was violated in any example of the Saviour's benevolent doings, in a sense of the word 'violation' which conflicts with the indubitable teaching of science concerning the unchangeableness of the laws of nature." "The record of Scripture presenting the narratives of Christ's miracles does not at any time represent our Saviour as interposing to stay for a brief period the action of fixed law, or to prevent the application of such law, in the history of a particular individual. In all these wonders of healing nothing more happens as to actual *result*, having a general bearing on procedure in the physical world, than does happen when a cure of a critical phase of disease is accomplished by some newly-discovered appliance at command of medical art. These two cases are essentially different as to *mode* of action, but they are strictly identical as to *result*; and this identity amounts to a demonstration of harmony with scientific requirements as these actually guide men to the discovery of new methods." *

Providences are seen on every hand. A man through carelessness lets fall a lighted lamp on board of a ship in mid-ocean: the ship takes fire, and three hundred human beings are lost and two hundred saved. God's providence connects itself with those that are lost as well as with those that are saved. If it had been the plan of God to save the ship and passengers, he could have cautioned the man who had the lamp, so that he would not

* *Relations of Science and Religion*, pp. 290, 293.

let it fall; but he did not do that. Sometimes he impresses souls, and thus saves them from danger and death. A man is walking on one side of the street, and the thought occurs to him to cross over to the other side; he follows the thought, and by that means is saved, for a house falls on the side of the street which he has left, which would have killed him had he remained there. A person may want to change his position in life, but God thinks it not best for him to change: he therefore throws an influence around him and keeps him where he is. A certain man is about to fall by a great temptation: he is checked by a divine impulse and held fast to righteousness.

"There is a government of men as moral and religious beings," remarks Isaac Taylor, " which is carried on chiefly by means of the *fortuities* of life. Those unforeseen accidents which so often control the lot of men constitute a *superstratum* in the system of human affairs wherein, peculiarly, the divine providence holds empire for the accomplishment of its special purposes. It is from this hidden and inexhaustible mine of chances—chances, as we must call them—that the Governor of the world draws, with unfathomable skill, the materials of his dispensations toward each individual of mankind. The world of nature affords no instances of complicated and exact contrivance comparable to that which so arranges the vast chaos of contingencies as to produce, with unerring precision, a special order of events adapted to the character of every individual of the human family. Amid the whirl of myriads of fortuities the means are selected and combined for constructing as many independent machineries of moral discipline as there are moral agents in the world; and each apparatus is at once complete in itself and complete as part of a universal movement." *

Divine providence does not destroy human freedom. We ourselves influence each other by example, argument, persuasion and the presentation of new truth; and so we hold each other in check or excite to a course of obedience without in the least injuring the will. We are thus in our sphere exercising providence, and surely God in his sphere may do the same. As far as the production of goodness is concerned, there is no difficulty; the difficulty is found in connecting the providence of God with the sin of man. We instinctively feel that God never can excite man to sin, and yet he may use the sin for a certain purpose. He did this in the case of Joseph and his brethren. The divine arrangement was that Joseph should go to Egypt, that there he might save much people alive; and the sin of his brethren was the means of sending him there. "They meant it for evil," but "God meant it for good." The crucifixion of Christ, as that links on to the determination of God and the depravity of men, is even more striking

* *Natural Hist. of Enthusiasm*, p. 128.

than the above case. The language is sharp and direct, there being no attempt to ease off the matter in the least: "Him, being delivered by the determinate counsel and foreknowledge of God, ye have taken, and by wicked hands have crucified and slain." Acts ii. 23. Here is sin having a share in the very redemption that was meant to destroy sin, showing how "God makes the wrath of man to praise him."

It is certain that the natural power of the creature is from the efficiency of the Creator. Man makes use of this power to sin, and yet God does not lead him to sin. The wicked have the gift of speech, but God does not incite the wicked to utter a falsehood by that gift of speech. He gives to a person physical strength, and by that physical strength the person overcomes and kills six men, yet God did not move him to act in that murderous manner. When the Bible says that "God hardened Pharaoh's heart," it means that he withdrew his Spirit from the man, left him to act in his own way, permitted him to fall by reason of the surrounding temptations—was, so to speak, the *occasion* of the hardening of his heart, while the *cause* was in the man himself.

As it respects *providential judgments*, we cannot always point them out. God's government over men in the Christian dispensation is different from his government over men in the Jewish dispensation. Temporal rewards and punishments are clearly marked in Old-Testament history, but the same method is not seen at present. Because twelve men were destroyed by an explosion we cannot say that they were more wicked than the men that were left uninjured. Some persons are punished and some afflicted, and to say which is the punishment and which the affliction is not always easy. If a murderer escapes justice, but is finally killed by an angry man, we see the hand of God in the judgment. The wicked, however, sometimes prosper, while the righteous suffer. Nations are punished and rewarded in the present life. Retribution to the individual is seen chiefly in the future life.

PART II.
DOCTRINE CONCERNING MAN.

CHAPTER I.
ORIGIN AND ANTIQUITY OF MAN.

THE theory of evolution forces itself on our attention. The fact that this theory embraces all the kingdoms of life, presenting a principle which binds them together, is an idea of great comprehensiveness, and may easily captivate minds of a certain order. It is admitted that there has been progress throughout the entire realm of animal existence. Looking simply at one of the sub-kingdoms, we can see an ascending march from the fish, reptile, bird, quadruped, to man. Although these orders are formed according to one type, that one type branches off from simplicity to manifoldness, so that when the highest creature is reached we are amazed at the intricacy and finish that meet us. It is admitted also that new features have appeared in certain animals, and that a high degree of improvement has been attained. "Adaptability," "environment," "natural selection," "the struggle for existence," have all been elements in the line of progress. It is not admitted, however, that the fish has become the reptile, the reptile the bird, the bird the quadruped, and the quadruped the man.

Darwin's "origin of species" is simply the *variation* of species. We all believe in the varieties of sheep, cattle, horses, dogs, pigeons—fully believe in the varieties of the apple, peach, pear, grape, strawberry. "It does not necessarily follow, however," says the duke of Argyll, "that because we admit the idea of the rock-dove and the turtle-dove and the ring-dove being all descended from one ancestral pigeon, we are bound to accept the idea of the whale and the antelope and the monkey being all descended from some one primeval mammal."* If the development theory were true, we should see classes of monstrous beings bridging the chasm between opposite species. Then, too, what is worthy of note, the first inhabitants of a group are not always the lowest. They are sometimes quite high, as if the chiefs led the way, while farther on the descendants sink in the scale. It is a fact also that different races have been swept from the earth at different times, thus interrupting the course of development. Then, again, in the Carboniferous period "feet with five toes appear in numerous species of reptilians of various grades. They are preceded by no other vertebrates than fishes, and

* *The Reign of Law*, p. 264.

these have numerous fin-rays instead of toes. There are no properly transitional forms, either fossil or recent. How were the five-fingered limbs acquired in this abrupt way? Why were they five rather than any other number? Why, when once introduced, have they continued unchanged up to the present day?" *

Huge creatures appear in the ancient seas and on the ancient earth, all at once, which can be traced to no ancestors. Independent creations are in this way facts of geological history. If animal development has culminated in man, why should we still have such a variety of animal species, as if no development had ever taken place? We should expect to see man reigning alone, the previous races being lost in him as their goal and grave. Quatrefages affirms that " not a single case of transmutation of one species into another has been scientifically established."

If man is evolved from the ape, the ape must possess the attributes of a man. We cannot evolve something out of nothing. The highest developed men have a brain of 94 inches; the lowest, 77. A brain below 65 inches is idiotic. The anthropoid apes have a brain that ranges from 28 to 32 inches, only one-third the size of that of enlightened men. How is it possible to connect the highest ape with the lowest man, since the one has only 32 inches of brain while the other has 77 inches? They

* Dawson, *Facts and Fancies in Modern Science*, p. 84

stand apart as truly as a tree on one side of a river and a flower on the other side. To evolve a human being from an ape is a physical impossibility.

When we view man as he is, he is seen to stand at an infinite remove from the noblest animal. He alone of all creatures upon earth can make a tool, kindle a fire, cook food, exchange one thing for another. Then there is the marvelous fact of language, which connects the human being with God rather than with the beast. Man does not differ merely in degree from the animal, but he differs in kind. He is the being who can sin, the subject of moral government, the heir of immortality. He can perceive the beauty of nature, the beauty of truth, the beauty of holiness. He has the idea of cause, the idea of the infinite, the idea of God. He can repent, can worship and can prepare for heaven. He can seek for the highest good, can labor with reference to an ultimate end, can aim to realize an ideal, and can benefit others at the bidding of conscience. He can think of a happiness that he has never known, a purity that he has never seen and a perfection that he has never reached. No animal has characteristics like these. Separate from all, and above all, the human being stands. "And God said, Let us make man in *our image,* after our likeness: and let them have dominion over the fish of the sea, and over the fowl of the air, and over the cattle, and over all the earth, and over every creeping thing that creepeth upon the earth. So God *created man in his image*, in the image of God created he him; male and female created he them." Gen. i. 26, 27. Surely, the appearance of man upon the earth is a miracle.

In regard to the *antiquity of man* we will begin with the discoveries that have been made in the mud of the river Nile: "Ninety-five openings were made into this mud, which has been accumulating for ages, and of these one or two penetrated to the depth of sixty feet below the surface. One shaft was sunk near the statue of Rameses II., and a small vase of coarse unglazed pottery, a saucer of similar material and the hinder part of a small lion in baked clay were found at a depth of ten feet, the blade of a copper knife at thirteen, a vessel of brown unglazed pottery at fifteen; fragments of burnt brick were brought up from a depth of thirty feet, and particles of baked clay from a depth of fifty-nine feet."

The question now is, At what rate did the Nile mud increase? Let the increase be estimated at six inches in a century. The baked clay that was brought up from a depth of fifty-nine feet would show, according to this, that men were engaged in making bricks about twelve thousand years ago. A piece of pottery has even been found at a depth of ninety feet. This would intimate that there were potters in Egypt eighteen thousand years ago. It has turned out, however, that this piece of pottery which delighted the skeptics was of *Roman* origin, and consequently it could only be traced back about two thousand years. This shows that all calculations with respect to the mud of the river Nile are of no value.

Glance now at the *flint* discoveries. Flints have been found at Abbéville in Picardy which were evidently shaped by men. They lay side by side with bones of extinct animals at depths ranging from twenty to thirty feet below the surface. "Flint implements have also been discovered in the caves of Gower, in a cavern near Wells in Somersetshire, at Icklingham in Suffolk, in the valley of the Ouse near Bedford, and at various other places in England." The inference is, that the men who shaped these flints lived during the same time as the animals with whose bones the flints were found. This would carry us back to the Drift period. I can easily conceive that the flints might have been washed into their present position by the wild force of rushing water. The gravel and sand of the Drift formation may have been opened up, and the flints which were upon the surface may have sunk to the place where the extinct animals lay.

We are told, however, that the remains of human beings have been found right beside the remains of the mastodon and the megalonyx, and so they must have lived at the same time. The bones that are found in an old English graveyard do not prove that persons were buried there at the same time merely because their bones now happen to be mingled together. We all know that the earth may sink at certain places, and it may be forced up at certain places, by some convulsion of nature, thus bringing together materials which at one time were quite apart. A rushing river may undermine the high banks on either side of it, and so a man that was buried not far from the surface, and a mastodon that was sepulchred lower down, may find themselves close together by this undermining of the earth.

It seems likely also that some of the gigantic animals now extinct really flourished during the first ages of human time. "We have no good evidence that the mammoth and cave-bear and woolly rhinoceros may not have lived up to the time of the historical Deluge." The Indians have a tradition of the appearance of an immense animal in the Ohio country. It is a fact also that "in the year 1799 a mammoth in an entire state thawed out of an ice-bank near the mouth of a river in the north of Siberia." This would seem to intimate that the creature lived within the bounds of the modern period.

The Swiss lake-dwellings are also brought forward to prove the great antiquity of man. "During the years 1853 and 1854 the water of the Lake of Zurich sank lower than it had been known to do for centuries," making it evident that people must have lived over the lake in buildings that rested on piles. By an examination of different lakes in Switzerland it was discovered that lake-dwellings had once been common. A number of articles of various kinds, showing the civilization of the people, were found—namely, "axes, hatchets, knives, lance-heads, swords, hammers, buttons, chains, fishing-tackle, shreds of flaxen cloth and round cakes of bread." It was noticed, however, that among one class of lake-dwellers the tools and weapons were made of *stone*, among another class they were made of *bronze*, while another class had them made of *iron*. This was supposed to point out three different stages of civilization, the people of the Stone Age being what is called pre-historic.

The argument for the antiquity of man from this quarter is of no great value. Herodotus mentions people who lived in lake-dwellings. Persons live in the same style at present in the East Indies, in Africa and in South America. And as to the Stone Age, there is no evidence that that is so very ancient, neither is there any evidence that the whole human race were savages at that time. During the first Chaldæan monarchy stone implements were used, and yet the people had reached a high degree of civilization. "The Stone Age exists to-day among certain savage tribes, and is contemporary with the steam-engine, the locomotive, the magnetic telegraph, that are types and indications of man's highest civilization in material things."

"The oldest men whose remains have been found," says Dr. Dawson, "are not of a different species from modern men, but, on the contrary, are nearly allied to the most widely-distributed modern race, while their great stature and physical power remind us of the Nephelim or giants of Genesis. The cranial capacity of these earliest men shows that they were as much lords of creation and as little allied to the brutes as their successors are. Further, when we place this fact in relation with the statement made by Haeckel, that according to the latest views of derivation lemurs or monkey-like animals of low type in the Eocene passed into apes in the Miocene, and these into men in the Post-Pliocene, the contradiction between this and the high type of the pre-historic skulls seems absolute, especially when we consider the unchanged character of the Turanian race from the Palæocosmic age to the present day." *

There is this point also, that the *beastly* theory of man's origin and the *savage* theory of man's primitive state lead to the view that the first men had no idea of God : they were fetich-worshipers. This is pure fancy. The facts of history go the other way. The earliest writings of the Old Testtament present to us a rounded monotheism. The idea of one God as Creator, Ruler and Judge is an idea that has swept the whole of time. Polytheism is a corruption of the true doctrine. Even panthe-

* *The Bible and Science*, Lect. v.

ism is theism disfigured by false philosophy. The farther back we go in the religions of India, China and Egypt, the faith is more simple and the idea of one God is more clear.

The philosophers of future ages will look back with astonishment at the popularity of evolution in the nineteenth century, wondering how scientific men were dazzled and deluded by it. The Bible statement, that Adam was " the *son of God*," has a grandeur about it, showing us at once the place he holds in the creation and his relationship to the Father of all.

CHAPTER II.

INNOCENCE AND FALL OF MAN.

THE first human being did not come into existence as an infant. Continued life would have been impossible in such a state of helplessness. Adam was created as a man, and was supernaturally endowed with knowledge and speech.

He was made in the *image* of God.

Constitutionally, this implies that his soul was immaterial; that it had the faculty of thought; that it had within itself a class of universal ideas pointing to cause, number, time, space, order, beauty, the infinite, right and wrong; that it had an emotional nature, with feelings suitable to different objects and different relations; that it possessed freedom of will; and that it was destined to an immortal life. In these respects it was like God.

Then, *morally*, there was a divine image. 1. Adam was filled with the *Spirit*. We might infer this from the fact that Christ, "the second Adam," received the Spirit without measure. No being is capable of communion with God without the presence of the supernatural. By reason of this the good live in a pure atmosphere. 2. The *mind* of Adam had a spiritual perception of truth, righteousness and God. The understanding being flooded with light, there was a clear consciousness. 3. The *heart* was full of love. With this it was completely centred on God and completely captivated with goodness. 4. The *will* had simply one holy movement, so that it expressed the entire soul righteously, keeping the law with a freedom that was pure and with a purity that was free.

How long our first parents lived in a state of innocence we know not. The time must have been short, because if it had been long habits of goodness would have been formed, and these would have kept them from falling. Certain writers have thought that inasmuch as Christ was in the wilderness forty days, so Adam and Eve were in the garden of Eden that time.

The account in Genesis respecting our first parents is history and not allegory. The temptation was not carried forward *in* the mind by Satan.

INNOCENCE AND FALL OF MAN. 69

His suggestions reached the mind through the medium of the serpent. Eve was found alone by the tempter. If Adam had been with her, it is possible that Satan would have failed. Great skill and cunning are manifested by the Evil One. He asks a preparatory question: "Yea, hath God said, Ye shall not eat of every tree of the garden?" Gen. iii. 1. Receiving the answer to this, he suggests a *doubt:* "Ye shall not surely die." Gen. iii. 4. As much as to say, You may be mistaken in regard to what God means. To die is fearful. You must not suppose that a being like God would inflict such a penalty. It would be contrary to his benevolence. The woman doubtless was arrested by this thought. She looked at it, turned it over: in this was her danger. If she had rejected it at once, all would have been well. When we argue with evil we are entering the trap. The tempter, gaining ground, says pleasantly, "God doth know that in the day ye eat thereof, then your eyes shall be opened; and ye shall be as gods, knowing good and evil." Gen. iii. 5. Here was a new view of the subject. Thinking that she may have been mistaken touching the divine command, she is the more ready to listen to the enticing words of Satan. Superior knowledge was to flash upon her mind, and she was to reach a divine standing. A sudden glare comes over her; there is a kind of intoxication. The fruit is good for food, pleasant to the eye, will make one wise. She is captivated; she yields; she takes the fruit; she disobeys God.

The woman fell, then the man, and so sin entered the world. Spiritual, temporal and eternal death is now the lot of our first parents. Their state in sin is just the opposite of their state in holiness. 1. The Holy Spirit has left them. 2. The mind is darkened. 3. God and goodness are lost. 4. The will is set for evil. Redemption, however, intervenes, and so the guilty are not driven away into everlasting punishment. There is to be a human race, and this human race is to be placed under remedial influences during a specific time.

What relation does Adam sustain to his posterity? The relation is very close: "By one man sin entered into the world, and death by sin; and so death passed upon all men, for that all have sinned." Rom. v. 12. "Even Infidelity plays into the hands of Orthodoxy. For example, the new positions on Heredity, asserting a common descent, laws of transmitted qualities and liabilities, character, etc., point directly to the great Christian doctrine of Original Sin." * The race is a unit. Men are not like grains of sand. The fountain being impure, the streams are impure. Adam is the natural and federal head of the race. If he had remained holy, his descendants would have been holy; but, breaking the divine law, we are involved in the consequences of his sin: "The judgment

* Prof. Henry B. Smith, *Lectures on Apologetics*, p. 191.

was by one to condemnation." Rom. v. 16. Of course we are not personally guilty of Adam's sin. Infants who die are saved by Christ. The persons who endure the agonies of the second death are *actual* sinners.

What is meant by original sin? It is not the first sin which Adam committed, nor the first sin which any man commits, but it is the corrupt moral state in which we are born. "Original sin," remarks Calvin, "appears to be an hereditary pravity and corruption of our nature, diffused through all the parts of the soul, rendering us obnoxious to the divine wrath, and producing in us those works which the Scripture calls 'works of the flesh.'" * "This original sin, however," says Augustine, "is nothing substantial, but is a quality of the affections, and a vice." † That is, it is not like a poison injected into the soul; it is rather a bad condition of the faculties. We are not born with sin in the same way that we are born with an intellect. We are like our fallen head in the following particulars: First, we are destitute of supernatural grace; secondly, destitute of a spiritual mind; thirdly, destitute of divine love, and inclined to self; fourthly, destitute of a holy will, and inclined to evil.

While there is danger of making inherited sin less than it is, there is danger also of making it

* *Institutes*, vol. i. p. 229.
† Wiggers, *Augustinism and Pelagianism*, p. 88.

greater than it is. The fallen nature of which we are conscious is blacker than the fallen nature we received from Adam. We have added to it a number of evil characteristics, a number of strictly personal characteristics. For instance, there is *pleasure* in our selfishness, *approval* of our waywardness, and a *choice* which has made the hereditary sin to be our own. If we go back as far as memory can carry us, we find that our *will* has adopted the native depravity, so that at no time are we conscious of gazing upon the solitary evil which came to us from Adam. It is difficult, then, to state it just as it is. While original sin is bad enough, we have no right to make it worse than it is—no right to force back upon a corrupt nature our vicious habits, and then call the whole mass of evil by the name of native depravity. Then, again, to say that we are not accountable for our bad states of mind, because we inherit them, is not to the point. Our bad states of mind, as we now have them, are colored and shaped by the action of our will. They are a part of our character, and so their demerit is our demerit.

In regard to the evidence of original sin—that is derived from Scripture and observation: " We are by nature the children of wrath " (Eph. ii. 3.); "Behold, I was shapen in iniquity; and in sin did my mother conceive me." (Ps. li. 5); " By one man's disobedience many were made sinners." Rom. v. 19. The fact that all men sin is evidence of a bad propensity. That all men begin to sin in a region back of consciousness and memory, is proof that evil is in us. It is frivolous to say that we sin by imitation. An infant will show temper and spite before it sees these characteristics in others. If character is formed by imitation, why have we not had a company of sinless men who acted like Christ? To say also that sin springs from the body is superficial. The angels sinned without a body. Sin in its essence belongs to mind. Enmity, pride and estrangement from God are states of the soul. That the body prompts to evil is admitted, but this is because the soul is godless. Even if we say that the lower passions and propensities are developed first, and by that means sin is introduced, we gain nothing, for that only proves that the governing power of the higher nature is lost.

Certain *theories of the origin of sin* may here be glanced at.

1. Sin is supposed to arise from the necessary limitation of the finite mind. There is thought to be a degree of imperfection in the fact that a being is finite, and that imperfection is viewed as sin or the cause of it. According to this, no intelligent creature can ever escape from sin, because no intelligent creature can cease from being finite: the Infinite only is holy. This is to destroy the nature of sin altogether, inasmuch as it is made necessary. It is out of the reach of the finite will; or if the will is allowed to have a part in it, the will sins

by natural imperfection. By this theory sin is taken out of the moral sphere entirely, and so its identity is gone.

2. Sin is supposed to arise from contrast. It is said that light implies darkness, health sickness, truth error, and good evil. What would virtue be if vice did not oppose it? Meekness, patience and self-denial presuppose evils that are opposed to these. Character would be tame and the mind weak if there were nothing to contend against. This view makes evil a necessary means of good, and, just so far as it does that, evil is made good. If humility is dependent upon pride, and love upon hatred, all moral distinctions are lost. Evil may furnish the opportunity for calling forth the noblest deeds of life, but it is not the cause of these. The energy of goodness is in goodness itself.

3. Sin is traced back to free will. The Catechism says: "Our first parents, being left to the freedom of their own will, fell from the estate wherein they were created, by sinning against God." This is no explanation; it is simply the statement of a fact. The question is, How could purity make choice of impurity? How could a perfectly holy being find a motive that would lead to sin? Inasmuch as the *free* will was a *good* will, how could it make choice of evil? The problem cannot be solved. It is a dread mystery. Sin is unreason, and so we can give no reasonable account

of its origin. We neither know how it *began* nor for what *purpose* it is here.

CHAPTER III.

SINFULNESS OF MAN.

I. SIN A STATE OF MIND.

SIN is not confined to individual acts of the will —acts which begin one moment and end the next: it is a *state* of the soul. "To teach that there is no such thing as a sinful state or condition or potentiality is an error which has deeply infected much modern theology in America and England."* When we say that sin is a state, we mean that there is an evil disposition or preference. The ambitious man who seeks power and position has a state of mind that is ambitious. The worldling has a worldly disposition, which rules him. The person who is avaricious does not merely sin when he refuses to help the needy: his avaricious heart is the seat of the evil, and the refusals to act kindly are only expressions of that heart. The revengeful man has his revengeful state of mind. His words of wrath against the person who has injured him are only the wild fruit of a bad tree. The particles of malaria which destroy health are from a malarious source, and it is the source of the evil

* Pope's *Compendium of Christian Theology*, vol. ii. p. 84.

which demands attention. Our idea of sin will always be deficient until we gaze at the fountain of depravity itself. It is the "sin that dwelleth in us" which leads to specific acts of transgression.

1. The sinful state of mind is *voluntary*. The will has two movements—one relating to evil *acts*, and the other relating to the *character* which lies back of the acts. The will adopts the depravity of the heart, forms a channel for it, and makes it to flow along that channel. The evil will in this way has mastered the soul. The unconverted man is where he is by his own choice. He will not turn from sin or accept of salvation; and this *will-not* shows that he has a voluntary habit of evil—shows that he is living in a *state of sin*. He says, "I do not want to adopt religion with all its self-denial; I choose to have my own way." That *not-wanting* religion and the *choosing* to have one's own way is simply the will acting in opposition to goodness. Impenitence and unbelief are voluntary states of mind.

2. As far as man is concerned apart from divine grace, the sinful state is *permanent*. Let one look into his soul at any moment and he will find the sinful state. Outward changes, outward moralities, have no effect upon the evil that reigns within. Whether one is awake or asleep, the state of sin is there. Place the unconverted man in heaven or in hell, and sin holds him—holds him for ever. And

yet it is of choice that the soul clings to it. There is nothing so fearful in all the universe as a bad will.

II. THE NATURE OF SIN.

Sin is not a mere mistake, nor an infirmity, nor a disease, nor a disorder.

1. Sin is a *departure from God.* Holiness is impossible unless the soul is united to God, so that to sin is to forsake him. God is *the* good; to leave that good is to apostatize. Estrangement is implied in the act of departing from God. The soul, not being easy in his presence, hastens away. The fall of man is the fall from God.

2. Sin is *lawlessness.* The point here is not the transgression of law by a specific act. To find the essence of sin we have to view it internally. Sin is therefore a *lawless* state; it is inherent rebellion. This inward lawlessness presses itself into the outward sphere, and there takes shape in lawless deeds.

3. Sin is *divergence from the right.* The person does not go in a straight line morally. We speak of an *upright* man: he does not incline to one side. A man of rectitude is a *straight* man. In turning aside from the right the idea is conveyed also of missing the mark. To whatever extent one fails of reaching the ultimate end of life, he sins. When character is perfect it is *finished*; the *end* is reached.

4. Sin is *selfishness*. It is not to be understood that all sin can be reduced to selfishness, or that fallen man never performs disinterested acts. The point is, that selfishness is a leading feature of sin; it sums up the chief part of it, so that man may be spoken of as emphatically selfish.

5. Sin is *idolatry*. Man takes the place of God. Let any sin be examined, and it will be found that the heart is given to it. The sin may appear small, yet, being accepted, God is rejected. That I have allowed myself to sin shows that I have chosen the finite instead of the Infinite. "What else is sin," says John Howe, "but an undue imitation of God? an exalting of the creature's will into a supremacy, and opposing it as such to the divine? To sin is to take upon us as if we were supreme and that there were no Lord over us; 'tis to assume to ourselves a deity, as if we were under no law or rule."

6. Sin is a *lie*. It is no wonder that Satan is called a "liar" and the "father" of lies. Sin is condensed in him in the form of falsehood. Moral evil from its nature is untruthful, and every person who sins is deceived. Sin is either viewed as a good or the means of good: in both cases there is deception. When once a man has forsaken God, who is truth itself, he most certainly lands himself in delusion. He is deluded about his character, about the great end of existence, about the way to obtain happiness. Hundreds of things are

right which he views to be wrong, and hundreds of things are wrong which he views to be right.

7. Sin is *spiritual indifference.* There is no real interest in that which is holy, divine and eternal, but quite an interest in that which is sinful, human and time-bound. There is ever an aversion to that which is good. When we come to measure the amount of indifference in souls, there is no fixed quantity. Like sin in general, it has degrees, some persons being more indifferent than others, and a person himself being more indifferent at one time than he is at another.

8. Sin is *malice.* Here it comes to a kind of perfection. Haman (see book of Esther), who would destroy the whole Jewish people because one man would not bow to him, is the personification of malignity. Sin viewed as malice has more of evil in it than sin viewed as selfishness. When goodness and God are hated, the hatred is absolute moral death.

The sin against the Holy Ghost may be explained under this head. Why this sin should be unpardonable, while sin against the Father and the Son is pardonable, may seem strange. The reason, however, appears to be found in this: The Spirit has the infinite remedy in his hands, and he applies it to fallen souls. His work is the *last work;* so that if he is rejected salvation is gone for ever. The sin against the Holy Ghost is thus *final;* the soul by it is cut off from mercy; it is subject to eternal condemnation. "In order to make man capable of committing it, evil must most thoroughly have pervaded him by a process of intensifying and spiritualizing. Blasphemy of the Holy Ghost, as it is the highest, so also is it the most spiritual, sin."*

The characteristics of the sin may be thus stated: *a.* The working of the Divine Spirit is *opposed*. *b.* He is opposed *maliciously*. *c.* The malicious opposition is carried so far as to reach the point of *complete obduracy*. The sin being pure malice, and fixed, it is Satanic. The fallen angels are shut out from mercy because of the complete malignity of their character, and the man who commits the sin against the Holy Ghost stands side by side with them. If a person is troubled lest he has committed this fearful sin, he has not committed it. The hardened soul which "has done despite unto the Spirit of grace" has no anxiety of that kind. It is stupefied and deadened, being mastered by eternal sin.

III. Entire Sinfulness of Man.

"Every imagination of the thoughts of his heart is only evil continually" (Gen. vi. 5); "There is none that doeth good, no, not one" (Rom. iii. 12); "They that are in the flesh cannot please God." Rom. viii. 8. When we say that men are totally depraved, we do not mean that they are as bad as

* Müller, *Doct. of Sin*, vol. ii. p. 478.

they can be, or that all are equally bad, but we mean that they are destitute of holiness and supremely attached to sin. They may have the virtues of honesty, temperance, prudence, patriotism, pity, benevolence and family affection, but they do not have supreme love to God, nor make his glory their chief end; so, the governing determination being wrong, all is wrong. Ungodliness reigns in the soul; the atmosphere is human; men have struck off into a cycle of their own; the leading powers of the mind are misdirected. There may be beautiful thoughts and sound thoughts relating to the Deity; motions of soul that proclaim the need of him; fears that arise because of him; strange prayers that wander around seeking for him; but he is not made the chief. In the divine sphere man is to be looked upon as a foreigner. He does not understand the language, has no ties of friendship; in loneliness he dwells. Man is even foreign to himself. The soul that has left and lost God has left and lost itself. The animating principle of a true life is dead. We behold the vacant temple, the altar still standing, the lamps without light and without oil, the paintings partly visible on the wall; but no worship ascends to Heaven.

Objections to the above view:

a. If I am entirely sinful, I have no conscience. It is surely plain enough that to know right and wrong does not make a man good. Conscience is not character. The ideas of heaven and of God do not make a man heavenly and godly. Satan has a comprehensive conscience, but he is the prince of evil.

b. It is said that men prosper, showing that God is on their side; consequently, they cannot be totally depraved. There is an inferior morality which belongs merely to this life, and which brings blessings upon those who practice it; but, while it tends to hold together society, it does not satisfy the divine law, and does not end in spiritual and eternal good.

c. Man has power to reform his character, and consequently he must possess righteousness. The reform is simply in the line of natural virtue; it never makes the sinful heart holy; and so the supposed righteousness is not that which is demanded by a perfect law.

d. A person affirms that he is not conscious of being totally depraved; he therefore rejects such a view of human nature. It should be understood that sin darkens the mind, deludes the conscience, deadens the heart; and, consequently, no man can form a right estimate of his own character. We must fall back upon the Bible description of human nature, as that is according to truth; and by that we learn that "the carnal mind is enmity against God, is not subject to the law of God, neither indeed can be." Rom. viii. 7.

CHAPTER IV.

FREE AGENCY OF MAN.

If man is a free agent, he is a moral agent; and moral agency implies the existence of a conscience.

1. Conscience is that faculty which perceives right and wrong; and this right and wrong are seen to characterize states of mind, motives, purposes and actions.

2. Conscience has an imperative power, or the sense of obligation; therefore it says by sovereign authority, "Be right and do right; you must neither be wrong nor do wrong."

3. If our character and conduct are good, we are praised; if bad, we are blamed.

4. The guilty mind looks to the past, when sin was committed, and to the future, when punishment is to be inflicted.

5. The same guilty mind trembles before God and wants a way of reconciliation.

In each of these divisions conscience has a twofold movement. There is the idea of *right* and *wrong;* the command to *favor* the right and to *frown* upon the wrong; the *praise* and the *blame;* the *past* sin and the *future* punishment; the *fear* of God and the *need* of reconciliation.

It is evident that conscience looks to moral qualities, and not to happiness, utility or the mere consequences of human actions. The right is to be followed because it is right; and this right is to be understood as the expression of the character of God, and not as that which harmonizes with the eternal fitness of things apart from God. All right action, therefore, is theistic.

We are to know also that no action is right, in the divine sense, unless it springs from a holy heart. A holy heart, however, must express itself in an outward act that is suitable in the circumstances, for if it is not suitable it will be wrong. If a good intention were all that was necessary in order to make an action good, we might steal and kill if we only believed that these were for the glory of God. We can no more change wrong into right than we can change error into truth by mere sincerity.

Natural ability necessarily belongs to free agency. There are persons who object to the phraseology "natural ability," believing that it is misleading in its influence. The thing intended, however, by the language is of great moment, lying as it does at the very basis of moral obligation. Natural ability simply points to the fact that man is created with all the faculties of an accountable being. He is capable of reasoning, remembering and perceiving first truths. He has an emotional nature also, and a will that can choose or refuse. Thus, the mind is a power working out in different directions—a power that is natural. Hence we use the language " natural ability," this being the birthright of every soul. Take away any of the faculties, and man would not be accountable. If a person is blind and deaf, he is not to be blamed because he cannot see and hear. Whether my soul be little or large by nature, I can give account only according to what it is, or according to what it might be by faithful development. I shall not be punished because I do not foreknow, as I have not the natural power to foreknow. All this is reasonable. God demands of us constant obedience because we have all the faculties which are necessary to obedience.

It is to be noted, however, that while fallen man has natural power, he has no inclination to use this for the attainment of holiness. He is consequently spoken of as in a state of *moral inability*. This does not mean that he lacks power to live what is called a *moral life*, for we may go to a great extent in that direction; but it means that he lacks spirituality of mind, being "dead in trespasses and sins." God, angels and glorified saints are *morally* unable to sin, and so it is certain that they will always be holy. Impenitent men and lost spirits are morally unable to be holy, and so it is certain that they will always sin. However great natural power may be, it never will break up moral inability. Man can rush into sin, but he cannot restore himself to holiness. Nations may reach a high degree of civilization by the simple working of natural power, and with a fair system of ethics they may have a fair morality; but with all this they are still godless nations.

We come now to *free will.* That we are voluntary beings is not a theory; it is a matter of consciousness. The race can never be made to believe that men lie and cheat with the same kind of necessity that winds blow and fire burns. Such necessity would make sin and holiness to be impossible. It gives men the right to plunge into all kinds of evil. A Reign of Terror is the result of such teaching. By free will is meant *the power to choose.* When I purpose to do anything whatsoever, I am free. When I refuse to do any wicked act, that refusal shows that I am free. The sun shines, the river flows to the ocean, and the law of gravitation works with great exactness, yet there is no choice in either, and so no freedom.

Certain writers speak of the liberty of indifference: the will does not incline to one side or the other; it is in a state of equilibrium. This may do for a stone, but not for a man. If a person does not incline to good or evil, he is out of the reach of moral reckoning. I am inwardly free when I can put forth a choice, and outwardly free when I am not hindered from carrying out that choice. If I check my appetites, desires, griefs, and even my nervousness, I am exercising my will. If I hold myself to duty in spite of great suffering, I am showing a high degree of will. In the leading preferences of the soul, whether they relate to sin or holiness, to self or God, there is a movement of the will. This personal faculty holds sway over a larger empire than most men are aware of. It encircles the soul, and even works beneath the plane of consciousness. Its first choice is not known to any mortal; it is thus in part prehistoric. As the mind is constantly thinking, so the will is constantly choosing.

What is the relation of *motives* to the will? The relation is fundamental. There are men who say that the will acts, at times, without a motive, and yet what value can we attach to an act that has neither aim nor reason? It must be very much like a ship that is simply floating on the ocean, having no port in view.

In every act of the will there are two motives—one that centres in the object chosen, called an objective motive; and the other that centres in the soul that makes the choice, called a subjective motive. For instance, I decide to go to Europe, wanting greatly to see the different countries of that part of the world. The attractions of Europe form the objective motive, and the desire to witness these is the subjective motive. The subjective motive may include the thoughts, feelings and tendencies which lead to volition; in fact, it may include everything which prompts the will to go in a particular direction. It is thus frequently complex instead of single.

Each man is influenced by leading states and ultimate conclusions of the mind. I am walking along the road, for instance, on a certain day when traveling is bad. I look from side to side to see which part is freest from water. Taking in the situation, I cross from point to point, and do this many times while on the way. If you were to ask me why I keep changing, I would answer that I keep changing because it is *best* to do so. The idea that it is best is the motive that prompts me. I attend church Sabbath after Sabbath You ask me why I am so particular. I am so particular because I want to obey God. The wanting to obey God is the motive that governs me. Sometimes a man chooses a course that is agreeable to him. The agreeable is the motive, and yet the course may be sinful.

Whether it is the strongest motive which leads to volition is of no importance. It is enough that there is a motive which is the antecedent of choice, call it by what name we please. A motive that is weak to one man is strong to another, this depending a good deal upon the mind and character of the individual.

Is the *efficient cause* of action found in the motive or in the will? Strictly speaking, it is found in the *person who wills*. There are writers who talk about the will as if it were a kind of *soul*. They are fierce in upholding what they call the self-determining power of the will, when it is evident that they mean the self-determining power of the *mind;* the word *self* pointing to the creaturely spirit in its totality. The will may be connected with thought, as when I deliberate; and with feeling, as when I love; but this does not prove that the will thinks and feels. The *reason* why the will acts in one way, and not in another, is found in the motive. Although efficiency may belong to the will, inasmuch as it is the centre of personality, yet it will not put forth a specific act unless a specific motive directs it. The power which belongs to a seed is found in its germ, but that power will not show itself in growth unless soil and moisture, air and heat, are supplied as conditions. The will in the same way will not strike out in particular directions unless the particular occasions are provided.

Does the will possess the power of contrary choice? Certainly, a man may change his mind hundreds of times in a week, and he may do things on one day which on the day previous he did not intend to do. No one denies this. But, the motives and circumstances remaining the same, can he put forth a different choice?

In one sense he cannot. How can the power go forth when no new reasons call for it? The person cannot go east and west at the same time. As the will is not an independent faculty, but is conditioned by motives, he can only take the course which these point out; and as the motives are not foreign to him, but express his own mind, he cannot escape from himself.

In another sense, however, we can say that man

has the power of contrary choice. Why does he feel guilty when he does wrong if he does not have natural power to the contrary? This may be admitted in order to uphold man's accountability to God; yet the difficulty with the fallen soul is that it has neither heart nor will to use its natural power in the way of pure obedience. Man could do differently *if he desired*, but *he does not desire*. Of course the evil disposition is his sin, and will be his sin for ever. If God changes the evil disposition, there is a power of contrary choice which is holy: in that alone there is hope.

CHAPTER V.

IMMORTALITY OF MAN.

1. THE human conscience and the divine justice demand a future state of being. The soul looks into eternity and descries a doom which is to come upon the wicked. So long as there is a guilty conscience, so long will there be a belief in immortality. Men in all countries have been forced to think of an evil that would meet them after death. An argument that would quiet the cold intellect would not quiet the fiery conscience. The belief in immortality is very much like the belief in God—each is wellnigh universal, and each springs mainly out of our moral nature. The fallen soul even tells

of coming bliss as well as coming woe. "As every one's conscience is, so in his heart he conceives hope or fear."

Then, looking at the justice of God, what shall we do with those who have destroyed the innocent if there be no punishment hereafter? It never can be made right for millions of the good to suffer or die by the hands of others while the guilty are allowed to escape. There must be another state of existence where the righteous and the wicked shall be treated according to their character.

2. The present life is not commensurate with the boundless aspirations of the soul; therefore a future state is necessary. There is that in man which runs out to the infinite and the eternal, and which compels the soul to be dissatisfied with what it finds here. The beast is contented with the satisfaction of its appetites, while the enlightened man is sickened with earthly good. The disappointed spirit therefore darts off and lives in the future, or it creates an ideal world into which it enters, hoping to find there the treasure which it needs. Assuredly, the unquenchable desires of the soul point to an everlasting state of being, where objects better adapted to it will be found, and where the hungry nature of man shall beg no more in vain.

3. The fitness of the mind for an eternal progress is evidence for an eternal existence. The brute creature goes so far in development, and then stops; but with man there is no limit to progress.

However high may be our attainments during the sweep of ages, we can think of no point when the soul will come to a stand. A mind so obviously made for an infinite ascent was never designed to pass away when the clock of life strikes twelve. The last hour, rather, which consigns to the sepulchre the earthly brother of the soul, is but the signal of the morning watch of eternity, which bids the pure spirit begin its never-ending day of holy toil. "Would an infinitely wise Being give us talents that are not to be exerted?—capacities that are never to be gratified? How can we find that wisdom which shines through all his works in the formation of man without looking on this world as only a nursery for the next, and believing that the several generations of rational creatures which rise up and disappear in such quick successions are only to receive their first rudiments of existence here, and afterward to be transplanted into a more friendly climate, where they may spread and flourish to all eternity?"*

4. The training of man individually and collectively points to a future state. The fact that a sinful race are allowed to live upon this earth would seem to intimate that the present economy is one of probation, and that during the continuance of it the design is that man should regain his former state of purity, after which he enters upon another scene of existence in harmony with his perfected

* *Spectator*, No. 111.

condition. Wherever we look, we find a system of machinery at work in exact accordance with this idea. There is a remedy for sin, and along with this trials and temptations, showing that the world is a reformatory school. Let any one now cast his mind down the centuries of coming time and see the human family lifted up on a high platform of intelligence and piety,—what will be the conclusion from this? Not surely that it will sink into nothingness, but rather this, that, having gone so high, it is now prepared to go still higher. The ultimate design of a probationary course having answered its purpose, it passes away, while eternity becomes the possession of immortal men. To suppose that a world of beings moving onward till a certain goal is reached is then snuffed out of existence is a thought more like madness than anything else.

5. The adaptedness of the soul to behold the manifestations of God is a proof of its immortality. It is a true thought of Martensen when he says that "all questions concerning human immortality may be traced back to our idea of God. The true conception of man is, that he is the organ of revelation for the Godhead."* Man is made in the divine image, and so he can see and admire the wondrous revelations of the Divine Being. God must, from the nature of the case, manifest himself for ever, for the time will never come when the Infi-

* *Christian Dogmatics*, p. 452.

nite will be fully manifested; and so the soul must be there to behold this endless manifestation. The soul must be there also, for the time will never come when a limited being shall take in the Unlimited. The more extended the manifestations of God during some remote age of eternity, the more extended must the soul be in order to grasp them. Man is for God, while God is for man.

These reasonings with reference to the immortality of the soul may be viewed as aids to faith, but not as the ground of it. Scripture makes all certain. Immortality is there stated as a *fact*, and not as a probability. "Then shall the dust return to the earth as it was: and the spirit shall return unto God who gave it." Eccles. xii. 7. The material part of man goes back to the earth: the immaterial part goes back to God to be judged. "Enoch was translated, that he should not see death." Heb. xi. 5. In him were linked together time and eternity. If men were skeptical in his days touching the immortal state, he was divinely honored as the visible proof of it. We read also that Abraham, Isaac and Jacob found a place in the kingdom of heaven, thus teaching us that these men are not only residents of eternity, but that they are saved. Then, too, Moses and Elias appeared on the mount where Christ was transfigured, proclaiming by their presence the fact of immortality. In the eleventh chapter of the Epistle to the Hebrews there is a list of heroic saints, and they are spoken of as " a great cloud of witnesses," as if from the heights of glory they were watching us in our toil. The rich man who died and was buried is represented as in a state of torment, making it evident that he was an inhabitant of the future world. Christ seemed to embody in himself the doctrine of the other life, for he entered it through the gates of death, and then returned to us from it. And, as if this were not sufficient, he ascended in sight of his disciples to the realms of God, there to greet his people when they enter his kingdom. We know, still further, that both good and bad are to be raised at the last day, and that the good are to be eternally happy and the bad eternally miserable, thus making it certain that each man, body and soul, is to exist as such for ever.

There is nothing of "conditional immortality" in all this. If man is not naturally immortal, why should God raise the wicked from nothingness at the last day and then send them back again to nothingness? The fact that the wicked are raised and made to suffer eternal punishment is proof that they are immortal. The righteous and the wicked differ as to *character*, but not as to endlessness. Salvation is conditional, but immortality is not. "This is *eternal life*, that they might *know* thee the only true God, and Jesus Christ, whom thou hast sent." John xvii. 3. "The word 'life,' when used of the soul of man, means not only conscious being, but a normal state of being in the likeness, fellowship and enjoyment of God. In like manner the word 'death,' when spoken of the soul, means alienation or separation from God; and when that separation is final it is eternal death. This is so plain that it never has been doubted, except for the purpose of supporting the doctrine of the annihilation of the wicked."*

CHAPTER VI.

MAN'S NEED OF A DIVINE HELPER.

It would seem as if the fallen race of men were feeling round for some kind of a divinity whom they cannot name. Having no clear conception of what he is, they are groping about in the dark, if perchance they may find him. There is a peculiar thought wandering through the mind, and that peculiar thought is trying to express the name of the Great Unknown; yet it cannot do it. The whole is like a half-remembered dream, part of which we can tell, while the other part is lost. If we were to see a man in the midst of a desert, and he were moving round and round, not knowing what he was doing, we should be astonished. But, approaching him, and learning that he has lost his way and also his reason, he having had no food or water for many days, we now perceive that the

* Dr. Charles Hodge, *Systematic Theology*, vol. iii. p. 874.

man was really trying to find his way out of the desert, and, although he was moving round and round, that only showed that something was wrong about his mind, but it did not show that the conception of having lost his way was gone from him: his confused efforts told of the dim thought that still was there to guide him. It is much in the same way that we explain the strange working of the soul as it reaches after the Divine One. Seneca mentions an idiot girl who had become blind, but who did not know that she was blind. She knew that darkness was around her, but supposed that light was elsewhere. That idiot girl makes us think of mankind.

There is evidently a tendency in all souls that is *divine*. This tendency is not the result of knowledge, feeling or volition: it is back of these. The tendency belongs to the nature of mind, and is God-created. It can no more be destroyed than the instinct of happiness or the convictions of right and wrong. Men may plunge into all kinds of wickedness, and even deny the existence of God, but they cannot destroy the Godward tendency of the soul. All nations have had their heroes, rulers, reformers and wise men, about whom they gathered and through whom they hoped to find deliverance; but after a season they were found to be wanting, and the cry was for some higher and better one to come who would be able to set things right. However intensely human the race may be, the feeling at last is, that only one with divine powers can meet their case.

There is the fact of *loss*, which throws out intimations of the divine. Schubert, in his *History of the Human Soul*, tells us of a "Hungarian lady of high rank who, for the preservation of her beautiful skin, washed herself in the blood of young maidens murdered by her own hand." * That woman's loss was far greater than her all-absorbing selfhood. It is not that souls are deeply sensible of their loss, but it is that the loss does affect the mind, suggesting that something valuable has dropped out of it, and that only by the possession of some noble treasure shall it ever feel well. There is no communion with the Supreme Excellence. Hence the creaturely spirit is uneasy in the midst of its loneliness, wishing for some day to come that has no cloud and for some joy to smile that has no grief. The Great Inhabitant has left his palace. His kingly voice is heard no more. No princely table is spread. The royal guests appear not. The halls of splendor are empty. The once beautiful walls are soiled. The divine pictures are defaced. The golden timepiece made in heaven is out of order. The precious stones have been sold and the money wasted. The royal gardens are covered with weeds; only a few flowers are seen. The fountains that used to flow are now dry. The river of life that once was near has

* Quoted in Ackermann's *Christian Element in Plato*, p. 197.

changed its course. In the place where the chapel of the King stood is now " an altar to the Unknown God."

There is the feeling of *unrest,* as if the soul were praying for a Divine Helper. No circumstances bring peace, no truth quiets the mind. The soul seems to be lamenting its fate, trying also to communicate with another soul that forms a part of itself—telling that other soul that sin ends in death. There seems to be a voluntary soul that is proud, hateful and self-willed, and back of it an involuntary soul that suffers, fears and wishes for good, heading in its own way toward the Eternal Light, and looking through the mists of the dawn for the Coming One. This involuntary soul with its pantings is often wiser than the voluntary one with its understanding. Indeed, if men would but listen to this deep-hidden soul with its infinite yearnings, they would soon find the Deliverer of mankind. It seems to be standing at the very gates of life, trying to force them open, that it may catch a glimpse of the mercy of God. Man is in want, and so he is struck with a great discontent. From very weariness he sins, not seeming to know that the weariness is the result of sin. He is displeased with himself, and that makes it plain that there is a something with which he would be pleased if once he could find it. " Men think that they regret the past, when they are but longing for the future." The sharp cry for unlimited good starts an opposite feeling, and that feeling seizes a good that has no value. The great want of the soul finding no way by which it can be satisfied is broken up into a thousand little wants; and these, fastening on to a thousand little objects, try in that way to fill the rankling void within.

There stand around each human soul beautiful *ideals*, prompting that soul to seek after all excellent things. These ideals differ in number and quality in varied minds. These are not designed to be a good in themselves, but rather the means which may lead to the highest good. Many imaginative persons do not view them in this way. They rather fix their chief attention on them. They turn them into idols. They worship them. As these ideals seem to be reflections of God, and not God himself, fallen men are better pleased with them than with him. Hence we find cultivated persons exhausting their energies upon art, making it as beautiful as they can, that the beauty may charm every beholder. Then there are men who tell us that they are seeking after truth for its own sake; and when they find it they make it their god. "Ideals are among us, like the crown diamonds, of the highest value. It is thought almost everywhere, in all seriousness, that men cannot do better than manufacture ideals." The difficulty, however, is, that "idealists *think* the good, but they *have* and *do* it not. Their thought stands in a melancholy disproportion to their being and will; it stretches up heavenward, it hovers around above the stars, while the rest of the man lies stunted on the earth, and, from its incompleteness and weakness, is unable to accomplish its purpose." * In the religious sphere splendid ideals are splendid failures. What bright ideal can ever lead to the creation of a pure heart and a pure life? The finest ideal cannot heal the schism of the soul or give to a man the blessedness which he craves. The sinful mind is rather exasperated by its visions of eternal goodness. The feeling of need is deepened, but not satisfied. Man feels more thirsty, but there is no water of life.

Despair hovers over the sin-stricken spirit. Even the great moralists are hopeless. Cold, dead works cannot warm the soul into life. Seneca cries out, "No man is able to clear himself; let some one give him a hand, let some one lead him out." What a sad wail that is! It seems to be a cry for the Restorer of human nature to come, and to come quickly. Ethics and art, philosophy and religious rites, cannot sweep away depravity and guilt. Even the pleasant doctrine of hope ends in despair. It would seem as if every human method had been tried: *failure* is stamped upon each. Souls are sad, burdened, lost; denial is useless. "The old poets, in general, are full of lamentation, and Grecian mythology could not conceal its internal stamp of a certain amount of tragic despair." "No na-

* Ackermann's *Christian Element in Plato*, pp. 76, 80.

tion felt more than the Greeks the unhappiness arising from the weakness and sin of the natural man. An undertone of lamentation runs through the external splendor and joy of Grecian life from its beginning to its close. In every mouth we find the same sad cry, It were better never to have been born; and its fellow, Or to die as soon as possible."*

Man's experience shows how urgent is the necessity for a Redeemer. God must intervene. The Divine Helper has come. Souls are saved by his power. "If any one wants to be a philosopher, he must go to philosophers; to be a poet, he must go to poets; to be a painter, he must go to painters; but if any one wants to be a Christian, he must go to Christ."

* Luthardt, *Fundamental Truths*, p. 395.

PART III.

DOCTRINE CONCERNING THE PERSON AND WORK OF THE MEDIATOR.

CHAPTER I.

THE DIVINE-HUMAN MEDIATOR.

ALL God's works flow from a holy tendency of his nature. In all his acts he has pleasure. Love was always in the heart of the Eternal Word, constraining him to become man. Only one Word has God uttered, but this one Word reveals God, contains all things and fills eternity.

"The first steps of Jehovah Elohim, who seeks man at eventide, are the first steps of God the Redeemer toward the goal of incarnation." "He is from this time the centre of humanity, which crushes the head of the serpent. The faith of the fathers derived from this centre of the promise and of the Promised One the strength of hope and of sanctification in the struggle with the power of evil."* The Old-Testament appearances of God in a human form were preludes of the incarna-

---

* Delitzsch, *Old-Test. Hist. of Redemption*, p. 25.

tion, and the two rolls of promise and prophecy terminate in "the second man, the Lord from heaven." Abraham saw his day and was glad. He is the great Prophet who was to appear, the Messiah and Son of God. He is the Servant of Jehovah, the universal King; yea, the "Priest upon his throne." He is the Lord who is higher than David; the One who "is to be cut off, but not for himself;" the One who "makes reconciliation for iniquity." He is the Angel of Jehovah and of the covenant; the Lord who is to come suddenly to his temple. "Unto us a child is born, unto us a Son is given: and the government shall be upon his shoulders: and his name shall be called Wonderful, Counselor, The mighty God, The everlasting Father, The Prince of Peace." Isa. ix. 6. The Old-Testament is really "the book of the generation of Jesus Christ."

The want of the race has been to find a way by which the divine could meet the human. If such a way could be found, man would be encouraged to approach the Being he has offended. In the Brahmanic system Vishnu is addressed by the gods in these words: "Take upon you a human body, and draw out this thorn from the world; for none but you, among the inhabitants of heaven, can destroy this sinner."* In this we have a hint of the incarnation as far as pantheism could give it to us. "Christianity gives expression to that which

* Pressensé, *Religions before Christ*, p. 60.

all religions seek; it embraces within itself whatever is true in heathenism and Judaism; but not less that the idea of the God-man, which so peculiarly characterizes Christianity, has not emerged from without Christianity, but wholly from within it. To Christianity this idea is original and essential. The beginning was the fact, and the fact gave the knowledge."*

That Christ was a *man* is not questioned. He was born of a woman; he increased in wisdom; he prayed; he was tempted; his soul was exceeding sorrowful; he cried out in agony because God had forsaken him. He must be God, however, as well as man, to be of any use to us.

I. CHRIST SEEN TO BE DIVINE FROM HIS NAMES, ATTRIBUTES AND WORKS, AND THE WORSHIP PAID TO HIM.

1. *Divine names* are applied to Christ: "In the beginning was the Word, and the Word was with God, and the Word was God;" "And the Word was made flesh, and dwelt among us, and we beheld his glory, the glory as of the only-begotten of the Father, full of grace and truth." John i. 1, 14. Here is a person who was *with* God in the past eternity, and at the same time *is God:* this person also assumes human nature. He is thus both God and man. In the Epistle to the Romans we have these words: "Of whom as concerning the

---

* Dorner, *Doct. of the Person of Christ*, vol. i. p. 45.

flesh Christ came, who is over all, God blessed for ever." Rom. ix. 5. That is, as to his lower nature he is human, but as to his higher nature he is divine. Then this explicit sentence: "Unto the Son he saith, Thy throne, O God, is for ever and ever." Heb. i. 8.

2. Christ possesses *divine attributes:* "Before Abraham was, I am." John viii. 58. Not before Abraham was *I was,* although that would show pre-existence. He uses the present tense, intimating that with him there is an eternal *now.* No wonder the Jews attempted to kill him, because he had claimed equality with God. He is omnipotent: "I have power to lay down my life, and I have power to take it again." John x. 18. The "I" can refer neither to the body nor to the soul: it must therefore refer to the divine nature of Christ. He is omniscient: "Lord, thou knowest all things; thou knowest that I love thee." John xxi. 19. He is unchangeable: "Jesus Christ, the same yesterday and to day and for ever." Heb. xiii. 8. We never speak of any finite being in that way. He is omnipresent: "Where two or three are gathered together in my name, there am I in the midst of them" (Matt. xviii. 20); "Lo, I am with you alway, even unto the end of the world." Matt. xxviii. 20. It is not possible for any human leader to be present with his scattered followers everywhere and always.

3. Christ performed *divine works.* We think

of his miracles, but it is not so much his miracles which show divinity as it is the *manner* in which he performed them. The apostles say when they would cure a lame man, "In the name of Jesus Christ of Nazareth rise up and walk." Acts. iii. 6. But when the Saviour would cure one in like circumstances his language is, "Arise, and take up thy couch, and go unto thine house." Luke v. 24. Here all is direct; he had the source of power in himself, while the apostles were merely the medium through which the power showed itself. Christ will also raise the dead and judge the world—acts which only God can perform.

4. Christ is an *object of worship:* "All men should honor the Son, even as they honor the Father" (John v. 23); "And when he bringeth in the first-begotten into the world, he saith, And let all the angels of God worship him." (Heb. i. 6); "And I beheld, and I heard the voice of many angels round about the throne, and the beasts, and the elders: and the number of them was ten thousand times ten thousand, and thousands of thousands; saying with a loud voice, Worthy is the Lamb that was slain to receive power, and riches, and wisdom, and strength, and honor, and glory, and blessing." Rev. v. 11, 12.

II. DO NOT THE WORDS, "SON OF MAN," AS USED BY CHRIST, IMPLY DIVINITY?

Some writers think that the language simply

means that Christ was the *ideal* man. No doubt he was the Man of men, the archetypal Man, brighter than the brightest of the sons of men. But this does not furnish us with the striking element of the phrase. When Christ calls himself "the Son of man," he means to teach us that he was in a state of *humiliation*. He had left a condition that was very high for one that was very low. He did not merely become a man, but he took the *servant state* of man. Hence the language, "The foxes have holes, and the birds of the air have nests; but the Son of man hath not where to lay his head" (Matt. viii. 20); "The Son of man came not to be ministered unto, but to minister, and to give his life a ransom for many." Matt. xx. 28. The fact of abasement, as seen in those verses, is seen also in this passage: "Being found in fashion as a man, he humbled himself, and became obedient unto death, even the death of the cross." Phil. ii. 8. We are not to understand that the humiliation of Christ was the act of his human nature, as if from princely manhood he had plunged into want, because that would convey the idea that he had existed as man before he came to this earth. He was always in a low condition here. Hence it was the Son of God who became the Son of man.

There is *divinity* in the language when once we reach the heart of it. We have this peculiar sentence: "The Son of man which is in heaven." John iii. 13. Certainly, the human nature of

Christ could not be in heaven and on earth at the same time. But as the human nature was necessarily connected with the divine in the one personality, the God-man could speak of himself as in heaven and on earth at the same time. We can say that Christ is everywhere, but we cannot say that the human soul and body of Christ are everywhere. When God became man, man did not become God, as that would make two divine Beings. Besides, if the human nature had really become divine, there is no human nature of Christ in existence. Passing this thought aside, then, we have the words, "The Son of man hath power on earth to forgive sins." Mark ii. 10. This appeared to the Jews as claiming divinity; for they say, "Who can forgive sins but God only?" "The Son of man is Lord also of the sabbath." Mark ii. 28. Not even a sinless man would venture to speak in that way. "Hereafter shall ye see the Son of man sitting on the right hand of power, and coming in the clouds of heaven." Matt. xxvi. 64. This statement created such a commotion that "the high priest rent his clothes, saying, He hath spoken blasphemy." Matt. xxvi. 65. Yes: Christ either blasphemed or he is God. He once asked his disciples, "Whom do men say that I, the Son of man, am?" "Simon Peter answered and said, Thou art the Christ, the Son of the living God." Matt. xvi. 13, 16. This answer was approved. Thus we have a divine-human Redeemer.

We meet now this question: Did any change take place in the divine nature when the Son of God became the Son of man? No. God may be spoken of as being in the material universe as well as in every human being, and yet there is no change because he is thus connected with matter and man. When it is said that Christ "made himself of no reputation," or *emptied* himself, that does not imply any change in the nature of God. It simply shows the greatness of Christ's condescension. If the Son of God when upon earth was emptied of his divine nature, he was nothing but a man, and as such he could do nothing to save man. God can do many things, but surely he cannot divest himself of his deity. He may not use all his power in given circumstances—in fact, he never will use all his power—but that is a different thing from setting aside his attributes. To make Christ a man with the divine left out is to make him an abnormal being. The *personality* of the Redeemer centres in the *divine*, and not in the human, so that we cannot even conceive of the man Christ Jesus apart from the divine. The Son of God did not join himself to a *man*, as that would give us *two persons*, but he assumed our *nature;* hence we speak of him as a *divine-human* person. Whatever of mystery is connected with this view, it is the mystery of transcendent truth. God in himself and in his relation to the universe is no less mysterious.

Individuals may use the language, "God in

Christ," and mean no more than that Christ was a man filled with God. They may say that Jesus was a *divine* man—that is, he possessed higher divine gifts than all other men—but they do not believe in the strict *deity* of Christ. Persons may even speak of the "incarnate God," and yet mean simply that God dwells in every human being. This may be intended to teach a form of divine immanence— God in all men and all men in God—or it may be nothing but pantheism. Strauss says: "Humanity is the union of the two natures—God become man, the Infinite manifesting itself in the finite, and the finite spirit remembering its infinitude." "It is Humanity that dies, rises and ascends to heaven." *
Here there is no incarnation of the second person of the Godhead : it is the human race in its totality that is incarnate. There is an old exploded theory which has been trying again to force itself into notice—namely, this: that God entered a *human body*. In such a case there is no man at all, for a body without a soul is not a man. There is a theophany, but nothing more. The theory gives us the startling thought that "God died." Those who adopt this view may be emphatic in their belief of the *divinity* of Christ. The belief, however, simply centres in *God* as the one who inhabited a human body. There was no real *person* of Christ. The doctrine is deistic.

Many Christians are at a loss to understand how

* *Life of Jesus*, vol. ii. p. 895.

the Saviour could be tempted. I will therefore add a few thoughts touching that point.

Adam, though holy, was tempted. Christ, though holy, can be tempted also. Remember that Christ was a *man* as well as God. a. There is reason to think that he was tempted at the beginning of his moral history. At that beginning there were no moral habits to hold him. The spiritual principle, therefore, was not as powerful as it was afterward. At the initial point, then, he was tested. It was passed safely. b. Christ had an æsthetic nature, and so he was influenced by scenes of beauty and grandeur. As his mission was redemptive, he must not allow these secondary matters to carry him away. In a lower sphere Howard was so much occupied in visiting dungeons that he had no time to regale his taste with the splendors of nature and art. c. As Christ had a body that was weak, he could be tempted to spend too much time in rest and recreation. Even sleep, though necessary, might be carried to an extreme. d. Christ was tempted by hunger. He could feed five thousand, but he must not satisfy his own cravings. A vast amount of sin has arisen from the bodily appetites. Christ controlled his. e. The Redeemer had divine power, but that must not be used to make his life more pleasant. As man's Saviour his position was that of want, self-denial and dependence, and so he must hold himself to these. f. It was a trial to Christ to live in the midst of so much wickedness.

His absolutely pure nature shrank from surrounding evil. It would seem as if he would long to be away. *g.* Christ gained but little sympathy, and that was a trial. He was even viewed as an impostor. His professed friends did not understand him. At the trying hour they left him. *h.* Christ was tempted by the greatness of his sufferings. He could not love pain; no one can love it. His human nature was torn to the utmost limit of endurance. The intensity of his agony we cannot measure. If he had given way all would have been lost.

Thus, Christ was tempted at many points and in many ways. What we are accustomed to call temptations are trifles in comparison with his. The first man fell through a single movement of Satanic influence: the second man fell not, though that Satanic influence was thrown over him during the great crises of his life.

CHAPTER II.

THE ATONEMENT OF THE MEDIATOR.

As the covenant of works made with Adam was broken, the race became a race of sinners, so that not one of the human family can now be saved by the law. A *covenant of redemption*, however, was formed between the Father and the Son. In this the Son agreed to be the surety of a select people given to him by the Father, he being willing to assume human nature, keep the law and suffer, so as to deliver these persons from sin and misery. Evidence of such a redemptive contract is found in these passages : " I have finished the work which thou gavest me to do" (John iv. 34); "This is the Father's will which hath sent me, that of all which he hath given me I should lose nothing, but should raise it up again at the last day" (John vi. 39); " I pray not for the world, but for them which thou hast given me." John xvii. 9. There is now the *covenant of grace.* Under this covenant salvation is offered by God to men upon the condition of faith; showing that we are living under a gracious economy.

The idea of atonement is rooted in human nature, and the idea of propitiatory sacrifice has taken a firm hold of the race. Thus, when the ancient Egyptians were about to sacrifice the animal which had been selected, Herodotus tells us that "the priests lead the victim, marked with their signet, to the altar, and, setting the wood alight, pour a libation of wine upon the altar in front of the victim, and at the same time invoke the god. Then they slay the animal, and, cutting off his head, proceed to flay the body. Next they take the head and heap imprecations on it. The imprecation is to this effect: They pray that if any evil is impending either over those who sacrifice or over universal Egypt, it may be made to fall upon that head."* "Well known are the hecatombs of bulls, lambs and goats (offered by the Greeks) in Homer. Pindar says it is a Grecian custom to sacrifice all, up to a hundred." "The animal was struck with the axe, and its throat cut with the knife. The blood was received into a basin, and in part poured around upon the altar, a part sprinkled upon those standing by, that they might be absolved from their sins."† The entire sacrificial system of the world is an attempt to utter the word *Redeemer*.

On the part of fallen man the following things are certain: 1. The soul can neither blot out its sin nor destroy the memory of it. 2. It cannot make amends for the past by any faithfulness in the future. 3. It cannot sweep away the terrors of eternity. 4. It cannot harmonize itself with infinite Purity. 5. It knows that repentance cannot annihilate sin and guilt. 6. It knows also that mere pardon cannot quiet the troubled conscience. 7. It has no power to make itself holy and happy. 8. It therefore is compelled to look to a divine atonement, that thus the law may be satisfied, God reconciled, the conscience quieted and the heart cleansed.

As sin is demerit, it demands punishment; and as justice has eternal claims, it must have punishment or its equivalent. To be just or not just is

---

* Rawlinson's *Herodotus*, vol. ii. p. 59.
† *Bibliotheca Sacra*, vol. i. pp. 399, 401.

not a matter of choice. Moral distinctions cannot be set aside in that way. No amount of power can make it right to go contrary to justice.

Men have formed their ideas of an atonement according as they have looked at God as a Father, Governor or Judge. With the fatherhood of God an atonement is not deemed necessary, as moral beings are viewed as members of a family, the offenders of which need chastisement and pardon, but nothing more. With God as the Governor of the universe an atonement has been shaped to sustain the public good and to satisfy the general justice of the Ruler, but destitute of any retributive quality. With God as a Judge the atonement has been made strictly judicial. There are phases of the atonement which honor all these relations of the Divine Being, but yet we must go back of them, and must fasten our eye upon the moral nature of God, that there we may see how the atonement expresses and pleases that moral nature. God's infinite abhorrence of sin and his infinite love of holiness, along with the instinct to punish the one and reward the other, shows that the atonement is a necessity of eternal righteousness. Sin never can be trifled with, for to the extent that we trifle with it we trifle with goodness and God. "Without shedding of blood is no remission." Heb. ix. 23.

The atonement of the God-man is vicarious; that is, he took our place in law and suffered in our stead. "He was wounded for our transgressions, he was bruised for our iniquities: the chastisement of our peace was upon him; and with his stripes we are healed." Isa. liii. 5. When the animal was sacrificed in Old-Testament times, its life was given for the life of the offender. If there is no substitution, there is no atonement. If Christ's life and death were designed merely to impress men, then that life and death had no atoning quality. It is admitted that the work of Christ will impress us, but the fact of impression does not make the work atoning. It is atoning first, and the real impression is gained from that fact. We even admit that by means of the atonement the believer is to be made perfectly holy, yet it would be a great mistake to say that the atonement is simply subjective on that account. It is true also that the atonement upholds the divine moral government, but it does that because it first upholds the divine law. It is sometimes said that the atonement relates to principles rather than to persons: it relates both to persons and principles.

The significance of Christ lies in the fact that he is the *Atoner*. The Eternal Son entered into time as a redemptive person. "He came to give his life a *ransom* for many." Mark x. 45. His position in the universe is not like that of any creature in existence. Creatures are born or created by an act of sovereign power, it being impossible for them to have any choice in the matter; but the Son of God became the Son of man by a voluntary act of his own. We are not to measure him by common rules of creaturely obligation. He being wholly exceptional, the one redemptive person in the system of the Almighty, his duty is unique. To say that Christ was merely the great Teacher, the great Reformer and the great Martyr is to lose sight of his expiatory character altogether, making him to be nothing but a very good man. That he is the *ideal man* is true as far as it goes. But when he says, "I lay down my life for the sheep" (John x. 15), that is an ideal which is not in a line with any man whatsoever. Christ is always the Redeemer.

If we are asked what we really mean by the atonement, our answer is this: It is a satisfaction made to divine justice by the sufferings and death of the God-man. The entire life of Christ upon earth was one of humiliation, and so it is redemptive. Although the atonement is a satisfaction to divine justice, it is none the less a manifestation of divine love. It was love which moved God to satisfy his justice in this way; and the greater the price paid for the redemption of men, the greater the divine benevolence. "Justice is satisfied in its severities, and mercy in its indulgences. The riches of grace are twisted with the terrors of wrath. The bowels of mercy are wound about the flaming sword of justice, and the sword of justice protects and secures the bowels of mercy. Thus is God righteous without being cruel, and merciful without being unjust." *

* Charnock, *Attributes of God*, vol. i. p. 557.

Whatever value attaches to the punishment of the sinner, as great a value attaches to the atonement of the Saviour. All the judicial elements which enter into each are not alike, because the innocent can never suffer like the guilty. Christ had no sense of guilt, no feeling of remorse, no dissatisfaction, no despair; but all these are sources of torment to the wicked. If it is the nature of justice to demand that the sufferings of the substitute should be the same in kind as that of the guilty, then there can be no atonement. That we have substitution at all shows that it is not needful that strict identity be carried out. Still, it is our doctrine that the sufferings of Christ were a *substituted penalty* and not a substitute for a penalty. "A substituted penalty is a strict equivalent, but a substitute *for* a penalty may be of inferior worth, as when a partial satisfaction is accepted for a plenary one." * "Christ hath redeemed us from the curse of the law, being made a curse for us." Gal. iii. 13. The expiatory sacrifice of the God-man will more redound to the glory of justice than if the collective company of the saved had been left to suffer the due reward of their deeds. The value of the atonement is infinite, because it was a divine-human person who suffered.

The *intensity* of Christ's sufferings can only be explained by the fact that they were *penal*. The mental pain was that of complete agony. If the

* Shedd *Hist. of Christian Doctrine*, vol. ii. p. 373.

divine nature had not upheld the human, the human would have given way. Christ was forsaken of God: he thus felt a torment equal to the second death. It would seem, even, that his pure mind suffered more by the withdrawal of the divine presence than any sinful soul could suffer, because a pure mind can fully realize what that loss is, while one that is sinful cannot. The burden of woe, however, only pressed upon him for a short time. If it had been the divine arrangement that Christ should pass through many Gethsemanes and suffer many crucifixions in order to atone for the guilty, we should have been appalled; but as it is, the atonement is complete for all eternity.

Besides, if Christ had to endure the eternal agonies of the lost, it would be necessary that the divine nature should suffer: the limited human nature never could "suffer the concentrated punishment of the misery everlasting." We shrink, however, from the thought that God suffers. He is the absolute *good*, while suffering is an evil. It is therefore foreign to the divine nature. When we read of "crucifying the Lord of glory," that is simply transferring to the lower nature of Christ the attributes of the higher. I may say of a man with a wounded limb that *he* suffers, and yet the seat of suffering is the *body*, and not the personal mind. Certainly, "the Lord of glory" viewed as *divine* could not be *crucified*, because crucifixion has reference to the body. So also to "kill the

Prince of life" could not mean to kill the *eternal Son* of God.

We should be careful also to understand that the chief idea of the atonement is not that Christ should deliver us from *suffering*. That would look as if *happiness* were the great matter. We are delivered from *punishment, guilt* and *sin*.

As regards the *extent* of the atonement a few statements may be made. It is a fact that all men are living under a redemptive system, and equally a fact that the full punishment of sin is not inflicted upon any man during the present life. These facts show that there is a sense in which the atonement is universal. "Christ is the propitiation for our sins; and not for ours only, but also for the sins of the whole world." 1 John ii. 2. As the same atonement which answers for one man answers for a million, and the same atonement which answers for a million answers for the whole human race, it is difficult to see at what point it can be limited. As far as its nature is concerned, it is unlimited. If the redemption-price for souls were exactly proportioned to the number of souls saved, even as a debt is paid according to the exact amount due, it would be limited; but no one understands the atonement in that way. Have I the right, then, to tell any man that Christ died for him? I have such a right. Suppose that all men would accept of salvation if it were offered to them; is it great enough to save them all? It *is* great enough: "God so loved the world, that he gave his only-begotten Son, that whosoever believeth in him should not perish, but have everlasting life." John iii. 16. It may even benefit other worlds, if such need it and God so use it. Since all men receive certain favors because of the atonement, can I say it was intended for all? I can. Whatever God does he always intended to do. Will the atonement save all? It will not. The numbers of men who oppose the gospel show that it does not save all. We are to distinguish between the existence of a remedy and the application of it. The atonement is sufficient *for* all, but not efficient *in* all. As it is a fact that the Christian redemption savingly benefits only a certain class, it must have been specially designed for them. Hence we read that "the Church of God was purchased with his own blood." Acts xx. 28.

Touching the priestly work of Christ in heaven, we know but little. Whether the intercession of the exalted Redeemer is carried forward by words, by signs or in silence we cannot say. It is sufficient that we have the *fact* itself, because that fact is crowded with heavenly and divine meaning. That Christ is a *Mediator* as well as an Atoner is an important truth: "He is able to save them to the uttermost that come unto God by him, seeing he ever liveth to make intercession for them." Heb. vii. 25. The whole life of Christ on earth and in heaven is but one redemptive prayer. The infinite merit of the God-man is pleading for ever for the people of his love. The fact that he is pictured out in heaven in the form of "a Lamb as it had been slain" is a constant appeal to the divine mercy, forming a kind of sacrificial supplication—no word being heard nor kneeling posture assumed, but simply the fragrance of atonement beseeching most sweetly that God would bless believing souls. There is one thing about the prayers of Jesus—they are always answered. Favors reach us on many a day that have come from him. Intercession opens the gates of heaven to ransomed souls.

CHAPTER III.

CHRIST AS MEDIATOR BEFORE REDEMPTION—MEDIATOR DURING REDEMPTION—MEDIATOR AFTER REDEMPTION.

As we study the nature of God we can see intimations that he will come forth from himself. Almighty power is almost a prophecy of creation. The divine wisdom seems to demand a sphere where it may be manifested. The benevolence and blessedness of God suggest that various orders of beings will be called into existence. Omniscience and omnipresence make us think of a vast created system. Divine justice points to a class of moral agents who will be rewarded or punished. Then we have the mercy of God. How can that be exercised unless there is a class of suffering and sinning people? "Herein is involved the deep thought that love to what is below it has a mediatory significance."

I. The Son of God as Mediator Previous to the Kingdom of Redemption.

As far as we can learn from Scripture, God does not act directly in the work of creation, but he acts through the medium of the Eternal Word. "All things were made by him [that is, by the Word], and without him was not anything made that was made. In him was life; and the life was the light of men" (John i. 3, 4); "By him [*i. e.* the Son] were all things created that are in heaven, and that are in earth, visible and invisible, whether they be thrones, or dominions, or principalities, or powers: all things were created by him and for him." Col. i. 16, 17.

The second person of the Godhead is thus the one who comes forth into time and space, unfolding the divine glories and carrying out the divine purposes. He *mediates* between God and the universe; and in this high and comprehensive sense he is the *Mediator*. "He is the image of the invisible God," the One in whom dwells the ideals of all created things. It is the doctrine of the divine Trinity which gives to us the true doctrine of the divine system.

The mediatorial idea of the universe has been expressed by many leading minds. "In the Eastern Church it was the prevailing view to consider God the Father as the sole efficient cause of all existence; the Logos (or Word) as being the revealing and mediatory principle." Athanasius says, "The Father creates all through his Logos." Basil of Cæsarea says: "By the agency of the Son all spirits were brought into existence."* "Although man had remained immaculately innocent," remarks Calvin, "yet his condition would have been too mean for him to approach to God without a Mediator."† Lord Bacon expresses himself in this language: "I believe that God is so holy, pure and jealous as it is impossible for him to be pleased in any creature, though the work of his own hands, so that neither angel, man nor world could stand, or can stand, one moment in his eyes, without beholding the same in the face of a Mediator."‡ Bucanus has these words: "Even supposing man had continued in his original righteousness, he would still have needed this Mediator."§ Nitzsch is no less clear: "Christ had co-operated with the Father equally as Mediator in all the works of God (such

---

* Neander's *Church Hist.* vol. ii. p. 420.

† *Institutes of the Christ. Religion,* vol. i. p. 419.

‡ See his *Confession of Faith.*

§ Quoted in Dorner's *Doctrine of the Person of Christ,* Divis. ii., vol. i. p. 366.

as those of creation), as he even now does in the work of redemption." *

The principle of mediation is seen through the whole of nature, as if it were a reflection of the mediatorship of Christ. Both God and man act through the medium of second causes. The universal ether is the medium of light, and the air the medium of sound. Electricity is the swift chariot of thought. Heat conditions life, and gravitation mediates in the realm of matter. The senses are the mediators of all living things, and language is the medium by which soul reaches soul. The march of progress among all creatures is a march by steps of mediation. Laws, forces, typical forms and minds express the mediatorial idea. When we think seriously of the surrounding creation, it seems to be interceding in behalf of men, asking that the great Mediator may come in order to lead them back to God.

II. The Incarnate Son of God as Mediator in the Kingdom of Redemption.

The mediatorship of Christ has now a *redemptive quality* connected with it. The Lord of worlds has come to restore the defaced image of God and to build up a kingdom of love in the midst of unloving men. The God-man is Redeemer and Reconciler. He stands forth as the *Head* of the Church. All believers are united to him by a spiritual life,

* *System of Christian Doctrine*, p. 186.

so that Christ and Christians form but one mystical body. He is not merely the Chieftain of the new race of men; he is the organic centre. Christ "recapitulates" in himself the whole of redeemed humanity; not only taking this humanity up into himself as its Redeemer, but summing up in himself the ideal humanity. He leads the race back to its source and forward to its goal—leads men to God, who is both *beginning and end.* Theology is Christological because the Son assumed human nature, and the Father or the Spirit did not. The God-man is sovereign, by mediatorial right, of the *higher order of intelligences,* being "far above all principality, and power, and might, and dominion, and every name that is named, not only in this world, but also in that which is to come." Eph. i. 21. He seems to be the wondrous bridge which extends from eternity to the utmost limits of life, through which flow the rivers of the ages. Well may Ignatius exclaim: "An archive to me is Christ; my incorrupt Bibliotheca is Christ's cross, death and resurrection." And with Polycarp we may say, "The faith delivered unto us is the mother of us all; her eldest daughter is Love; her second, Hope."

The only person that opens the mysterious temple of the race and gives a full and final explanation of it is the Incarnate Mediator. "A complete system of truth must embrace both God and man, both time and eternity. It must have its ultimate grounds, beyond which our thoughts cannot reach— its ultimate ends, solving the problem of the final destiny of humanity; and it must contain in itself the powers by which it can achieve the ends which it forecasts as needed and best. These tests of a real and final system of truth apply, we hold, to the Christian system, viewed as centring in the person and work of Christ, and to that alone." * Even M. Comte is willing to admit that "the first dawning sense of human progression was inspired by Christianity." † He says also that "the most certain signs of conceptions being scientific are *continuousness* and fertility." ‡ Where has any system shown the fertility and continuousness of the religion of the divine-human Saviour? Its literature and its life and all embracing power speak for themselves. Certainly, the ultimate end of the race is not the attainment of knowledge and liberty, for these cannot banish sin from the soul. But when we see that God has given us a revelation of his will, has become incarnate in order to provide a redemption, and has sent his Spirit to apply that redemption, we behold a method that meets the state of fallen man.

The working of providence is in the interest of redemption. The history of the race has divine and human elements in it, as if it were pointing to the divine-human Mediator. The world before

---

* Henry B. Smith, *Faith and Philosophy*, p. 143.
† *Positive Philosophy*, p. 440.   ‡ Ibid, p. 447.

Christ and the world since are looking to him. The panorama of salvation is in process of unfolding. Picture after picture appears. We gaze at the cross of Calvary, on which the Son of God hangs as the central object; the Saviour ascending to the right hand of power; the exalted Redeemer on his throne; the work of the eternal Spirit in the hearts of the converted; the hastening on of the latter-day glory; the second coming of earth's King and Lord; the awakening of the congregated dead; the array of all mankind at the bar of heaven; the trial and sentence; the flight of the wicked to misery; the consumed world; the ascent of the righteous to the city of God; the end of redemption.

III. THE INCARNATE SON OF GOD AS MEDIATOR AFTER THE KINGDOM OF REDEMPTION HAS PASSED AWAY.

Redemption is a wondrous episode of Infinite Love. It will be the one glory that will never be forgotten by good or bad. Although the work of redemption comes to an end, the God-man will still be related to the unnumbered millions he has redeemed. "The Lamb which is in the midst of the throne shall feed them, and shall lead them unto living fountains of waters: and God shall wipe away all tears from their eyes." Rev. vii. 17. As during the past eternity "the Word was with God," so during the future eternity the Incarnate

Word acts with him. In the world of the saved there is "a pure river of water of life, clear as crystal, proceeding out of the throne of God and of the *Lamb*" (Rev. xxii. 1), showing that from the Mediator blessings flow to souls, and that he is the Minister and Monarch of a great people.

There must be that in the God-man which will give him a universal significance apart from any redemption. The simple fact that there is to be an *eternal God-man* shows that he must sustain some high relation to God's system. Will he not be the medium through whom the Infinite communicates with the finite? The God-man is at once the *revelation* and the *Revealer* of God. This double characteristic throws out upon the coming eternity a blaze of divine glory. The God-man is evidently the central Being of the creation, the One toward whom all eyes are turned. He is not merely "the Desire of all nations," but he is the Desire of all worlds. When we see that there is an eternal significance connected with the God-man, that fact shows that sin is not the sole ground of the incarnation. If the incarnation is only of use with reference to the redemptive economy, then at the end of that economy the incarnation must cease. We should thus have two absolute religions—one centring in the divine-human Mediator, and the other centring in the Divine Being. But having the God-man to be eternal, he is then the point of unity for the one eternal and universal religion.

While we fully admit that the incarnate Son of God is the only *means* of salvation, we must be careful lest we make him nothing but a means. Is it not more proper to say that the God-man is both *means* and *end?* There is assuredly a great theology that is yet to appear during the sweep of the everlasting ages; and equally true is it that a great Christology must unfold itself for ever and ever. We cannot imagine how much is wrapped up in the one doctrine of an eternal God-man. There is simply an impression on the mind that truth and life of a very high nature are to show themselves. As the manifestation of God must be endless, so the mediatorial relation must be endless. The Incarnate Mediator, then, will be the glory of eternity.

PART IV.

DOCTRINE CONCERNING THE PERSON AND WORK OF THE HOLY SPIRIT.

CHAPTER I.

THE HOLY SPIRIT.

OUR knowledge of the Spirit is not so extended as our knowledge of Christ. Even among the early Christians the Divine Saviour was more an object of study than the Divine Spirit. The tendency has been to think of *grace* rather than of the *Person* who brings it to us.

1. The *personality* of the Spirit. The language "Spirit of God" does not always refer to the third person of the Trinity. Take this passage as an instance: "And Pharaoh said unto his servants, Can we find such a one as this is, a man in whom the spirit of God is?" Gen. xli. 38. There are numerous places, however, in the Bible in which the term "Spirit" implies a person distinct from the Father and the Son. Christ says: "The Comforter, which is the Holy Ghost, whom

the Father will send in my name, he shall teach you all things, and bring all things to your remembrance, whatsoever I have said unto you" (John xiv. 26); "When the Comforter is come, whom I will send unto you from the Father, even the Spirit of truth which proceedeth from the Father, he shall testify of me." John xv. 26. If this language has any meaning, the Comforter is one of the persons of the Godhead. He is not the absolute Deity, neither is he an energy which comes from him; but he is a divine person distinct from the other divine persons. The masculine pronoun (*he*) is applied to him, and he does things which a person only can do. He loves, reproves, searches, reveals, teaches, guides, quickens, comforts, sanctifies. Then we are entreated not to "grieve the Holy Spirit." Only a person can be *grieved*. His names are striking: "The Spirit," "the Holy Spirit," "the Spirit of God," "thy good Spirit," "the Spirit of Christ," "the Spirit of grace," "the Spirit of truth," "the Spirit of glory," "the eternal Spirit."

2. The *divinity* of the Spirit. The proofs of his personality are proofs also of his divinity. Note, however, one or two passages: "Peter said, Ananias, why hath Satan filled thine heart to lie to the Holy Ghost?" "Thou hast not lied unto men, but unto God." Acts v. 3, 4. To lie to the Holy Ghost and to God is the same thing, as far as divinity is concerned. Then this text: "God hath re-

vealed them unto us by his Spirit: for the Spirit searcheth all things, yea, the deep things of God." 1 Cor. ii. 10. Here the treasures of the divine mind are revealed to us by the Spirit, as he only is able to explore that mind; consequently, he must be divine. In the prophecy of Isaiah we have these words: "The Lord said, Go, and tell this people, Hear ye indeed, but understand not; and see ye indeed, but perceive not." Isa. vi. 9. In the Acts of the Apostles the same passage is referred to in this way: "Well spake the Holy Ghost by Esaias the prophet unto our fathers, Saying, Go unto this people, and say, Hearing ye shall hear, and shall not understand; and seeing ye shall see and not perceive." Acts xxviii. 25, 26. Thus in one passage it is the *Lord*, and in the other it is the *Holy Ghost*, making plain the divinity of the Spirit. Then, too, the one sin that is unpardonable is the sin against the Holy Ghost, this clearly teaching us that the Holy Ghost is a divine person.

3. The *procession* of the Spirit. This is supposed to point to a movement of the Godhead equally mysterious with that of the generation of the Son. The Greek Church believes that the Spirit proceeds from the *Father;* the Latin Church and the great body of evangelical Christians believe that the Spirit proceeds from the *Father and the Son.* If the Son has no agency in this matter, it is feared that he will be viewed as *less* than the Father. Certain writers state that the Spirit pro-

ceeds *from* the Father *through* the Son. The doctrine has come down to us in this form: "The Holy Spirit neither generates nor is generated, but proceeds from the Father and the Son."

4. How the *work* of the Spirit is distinguished from the works of the other persons of the Godhead. "The *order of operation* among the distinct persons depends on the *order of their subsistence* in the blessed Trinity. In every great work of God the *concluding, completing, perfecting acts* are ascribed unto the Holy Ghost. Hence the immediate actings of the Spirit are the most hidden, curious and mysterious, as those which contain the perfecting part of the works of God. The beginning of divine operations is assigned unto the Father: 'Of him, and through him, and to him, are all things.' Rom. xi. 36. The subsisting, establishing and upholding of all things is ascribed unto the Son: 'He is before all things, and by him all things consist.' Col. i. 17. And the finishing and perfecting of all these works is ascribed to the Holy Spirit. I say not this as though one person succeeded unto another in their operation, or as though where one ceased and gave over a work the other took it up and carried it on; but on those divine works which outwardly are of God there is an especial impression of the order of the operation of each person with respect unto their natural and necessary subsistence, as also with regard unto their internal characteristical properties, whereby

we are distinctly taught to know them and adore them." *

5. The Spirit sustained a *special relation* to the *man* Christ Jesus. While the Lutheran Church has labored hard to clothe the humanity of Christ with divine attributes, the Reformed Church has endeavored to show that Christ as man was led by the Spirit, fully believing at the same time that he is a divine-human person. The human nature of Jesus was called into existence by the power of the Holy Ghost, and his soul was constantly influenced by the same Spirit. It is written that "the child grew, and waxed strong in spirit, filled with wisdom; and the grace of God was upon him." Luke ii. 40. The phraseology, that "the *grace* of God was upon him," is exceedingly suggestive, hinting to us that every moral being, as he comes forth from the hand of his Maker, is endowed with supernatural gifts; for if the *ideal man* was endowed with grace, much more will they who are less than he be thus favored, they needing the grace more than he ever could need it. Indeed, to begin existence with a holy disposition is impossible without the presence of the Holy Spirit; and if that disposition is to continue, the same Spirit must animate the soul. There are three passages which may be noted: "And Jesus being full of the Holy Ghost returned from Jordan, and was led by the Spirit into the wilderness" (Luke iv. 1); "The Spirit of

Owen's *Works*, vol. iii. p. 94.

the Lord is upon me, because he hath anointed me to preach the gospel to the poor" (Luke iv. 18); "He whom God hath sent speaketh the words of God: for God giveth not the Spirit by measure unto him." John iii. 34. Thus Christ was conceived, consecrated, directed, cheered and sustained by the Divine Spirit.

6. The Spirit may be viewed now as the *inspirer* of the Scripture-writers. "Holy men of God spake as they were moved by the Holy Ghost." 2 Pet. i. 21. In the Bible, therefore, we have an infallible rule of faith and practice. We cannot admit that the sacred penmen were allowed to fall into mistakes respecting persons, places, doctrines, precepts and events. Points are not always stated in full. Genealogical records are sometimes copied as they are found, although the records may show blanks here and there.

Absolute contradiction of one writer with another, or of one writer with himself, does not exist. The Bible has its value from the fact that it is "the word of God." An erroneous book is of no use to erroneous men. The recent discoveries in Assyria, in the Holy Land and in Egypt make it more and more clear that the Scripture records are authentic. A seeming mistake to-day is a truth to-morrow. Not a single new doctrine or a new virtue has been discovered outside of Bible-teaching. The most that we can do is to draw out and apply divine revelation. The more we are imbued with the Spirit, the better we shall understand that Book which the Spirit inspired. If I would see truth and God, I must be truthful and godly.

7. *Unusual gifts* proceed from the Spirit. Among these are the word of wisdom, the word of knowledge, faith, gifts of healing, working of miracles, prophecy, discerning of spirits, divers kinds of tongues, interpretation of tongues. Even bad men are sometimes affected supernaturally, as Balaam in uttering words of prophecy, and Saul when among the prophets. Skillful men are sometimes made also more skillful, and inventive men are sometimes led to strike upon inventions by the help of God.

8. The Spirit gives to all men "*common grace.*" The fact that God's "Spirit will not always strive with man," and the other fact that there is a sin against the Holy Ghost, make it evident that the finally lost have been partakers of grace. It is a matter of consciousness that the Spirit powerfully affects thousands of impenitent men—men who remain impenitent in spite of all the influences which are brought to bear upon them. Indeed, there is no telling how much mankind have been restrained from evil and prompted to deeds of virtue by the working of common grace. Conscience, the natural sympathies and the far-reaching aspirations of the soul have all been intensified by divine influence. This earth would be hell if it

were not for the energy of common grace. The fearful thing about the lost in perdition will be that the Spirit of God has left them. We can say, then, that the whole human race are now living under a redemptive system. The system not being legal, not a single man will reach heaven by works of law. Of course all men are under law, but, inasmuch as all men have broken it, they cannot be saved by it: grace alone saves.

9. The Spirit *restores men* to the image of God. Christ by his atoning work has provided an infinite fund of grace, and this is used by the Spirit in enlightening men, convincing them of sin, generating in them a sense of need, leading them to make a complete surrender of their souls to the Saviour, and causing them to advance in holiness till perfection is reached. The work of the Spirit has about it a most wonderful delicacy and finish. Our rough natures do not perceive its beauty and fineness. When he works through human agency, we begin to notice his ways; when he leads a man to utter a sentence or perform an action that blesses a soul for ever, we apprehend his power. If our tabernacle were pitched on the borders of heaven we should understand far better than we do now the mission of the Spirit. A feeling of awe steals over us as we think of his hidden work in souls. The solitudes of the mind are broken in upon by his presence. There is calmness and power. The night departs and the day begins.

"The Holy Ghost," says Dr. Parker, "is the *reasonable* completion of theological revelation, and as such his ministry is an impregnable proof of the reasonableness of Christianity. In the person of Jesus Christ truth was outward, visible and most beautiful: in the person of the Holy Ghost truth is inward, spiritual, all-transfiguring. By the very necessity of the case the bodily Christ could be but a passing figure, but by a gracious mystery he caused himself to be succeeded by an eternal Presence, 'even the Spirit of truth, which abideth for ever.'"* The Spirit is a kind of hidden Mediator—working *in* souls: Christ is an outward Mediator—working *for* souls. The mediatorship of both will be everlasting. The good will always study God through the God-man, and will always commune with God through the Holy Spirit.

CHAPTER II.

ELECTION—THE PERSONS TO WHOM THE SPIRIT APPLIES THE DIVINE REMEDY.

GOD does not treat all men in the same way. He leads some to the attainment of wealth and knowledge, while others are left to poverty and ignorance. Advantages or disadvantages meet one according to

* *The Paraclete*, p. 17.

the century in which he is born, the parents he happens to have and the nation in which he finds himself. The position of men as to climate and soil is equally varied. Then as to native endowments there is no similarity. No soul is like any other soul, and no human body is like any other human body. To say that God respects persons because he treats them differently is meaningless. He treats all fairly, never viewing the good as bad, nor the bad as good. If the mighty works which were done in Chorazin and Bethsaida had been done in Tyre and Sidon, they would have repented, showing that advantages were granted to the one class of people which were not granted to the other.

The doctrine of election is not needed to tell us that only a certain number of men will be saved, because it is clear that only a certain number of men are truly pious. The doctrine of reprobation is not needed to tell us that there are men who will be lost, because it is equally clear that there are men who live and die in opposition to God. That one class are chosen and the other not, simply explains the actual facts. Men have to accept of salvation and keep the commandments whether election is revealed or not. To say that election is confined to nations, and that the gospel call is general, does not express the whole truth. There are elect persons in the midst of the chosen nation, and there is an effectual call besides the one that is general.

By election is meant the purpose of God to save

a certain number of the human race. The choice of the persons is not conditioned by good works, because they have none; it is not conditioned by faith, because faith is the gift of God. Doubtless there are reasons in the mind of God why he selects one person instead of another. He never acts blindly. The reasons, however, are not revealed to us. All we know is, that God acts "according to his own good pleasure, and that he is infinitely holy, just and good." In order to save the persons he has chosen he leads them to repent, believe and become holy. As salvation is of grace from beginning to end, the entire glory belongs to God.

Rev. Joseph A. Beet, the English Wesleyan, makes the following candid statement: "With Calvin and Augustine, I hold firmly that salvation is entirely, from the first good desire until victory over death, a work of God and an accomplishment of his eternal purpose; that we should never have begun to seek had he not first sought us, and that our seeking him was the result of his drawing us to himself; that our faith is wrought in us by the word of God, and by influences which lead us to believe it; and that every victory over sin and self is God's gift to us and work in us." *

Proof-passages of the doctrine are these: "He hath chosen us in him before the foundation of the world, that we should be holy and without blame before him in love" (Eph. i. 4); "God hath from

* Quoted in *Biblioth. Sacra*, vol. xxxix. p. 204.

the beginning chosen you to salvation through sanctification of the Spirit and belief of the truth" (2 Thess. ii. 13); "Whom he did predestinate, them he also called; and whom he called, them he also justified: and whom he justified, them he also glorified" (Rom. viii. 30); "Who hath saved us, and called us with a holy calling, not according to our works, but according to his own purpose and grace, which was given us in Christ Jesus before the world began" (2 Tim. i. 9); "So then it is not of him that willeth, nor of him that runneth, but of God that showeth mercy." Rom. ix. 16.

Sometimes the doctrine of election is made to appear both repulsive and false by a bristling statement of it. The Confession of Faith has a sentence of this character: "Some men and angels are predestinated unto everlasting life, and others foreordained to everlasting death." A theological mind will understand this, but a common mind will be confused by it. God does not create men to damn them. Men are punished because of wickedness, and the decree is founded on the fact of *guilt*. The purpose to save is a *sovereign* act, but the purpose to punish is a *judicial* act. When a judge decrees that a man shall be imprisoned for life, he is imprisoned for life because of a criminal offence. To this no one can object. The Confession of Faith speaks also of "elect infants," as if some infants went to perdition. To avoid mistake on a subject of this kind, it should be distinctly understood that the belief of Presbyterians is, that *all* children dying in infancy are regenerated by the Spirit and saved through the redemption of Christ.

If all men begin life with what our Methodist friends call "gracious ability" and "full power of will," why is it that, as a matter of fact, all men have sinned in spite of that gracious ability and full power of will? Surely the grace that was sufficient has proved itself inefficient, and the will that was powerful has proved itself powerless. If no man is responsible unless he receive gracious ability, why not leave the whole human race in that irresponsible state, as in that case all would escape punishment? Millions of men, on this theory, are able to trample upon the law and the gospel because their nature has been lifted up to a proper level by gracious ability, and these same men land themselves in perdition as the result of grace. If this is the true theory, it is a strange one.

But what is this "gracious ability" which is supposed to be given to all men? It cannot be *holy ability* or a *new heart,* for if it were either of these it would be the same as regeneration—a thing which few persons will claim. Although gracious ability, then, may be a power bestowed on man, yet if it is not the implantation of a principle of righteousness, it leaves him still in the grasp of total depravity; and the query is, how a totally-depraved man can begin to love God supremely unless he has grace that will conquer that depravity. Sin cannot make choice of holiness. If vital piety makes its appearance in a man's soul for the first time, that vital piety is an *effect;* and, as every effect must have a cause, the only adequate cause in such a case is *God.* "Election is simply the application of the law of causality to the religious life." *

Men do resist the grace of God, and yet many such men are led to submit to God, showing that an influence was brought to bear upon them that was stronger than their resistance. The first convert of Dr. Duff speaks of himself in this way: "A twelvemonth ago I was an atheist, a materialist, a physical necessarian; and what am I now? A baptized Christian.... What a change! My progress was not that of earnest inquiry, but of earnest opposition. And to the last my heart was opposed. *In spite of myself I became a Christian.* Surely some unseen Power must have been guiding me. Surely this must have been what the Bible calls 'grace'—free grace, sovereign grace—and if ever there was an election of grace, surely I am one." †

It is a fact that men are usually converted in connection with divine truth, so that where the truth is not men are not usually converted. Thus, saving grace and the means of grace are in a sense linked together. Missionaries tell us that they find no godly men among the heathen. The theory of "a universal call," with "sufficient grace," amounts

---

* Prof. Smith, *Introduction to Theology,* p. 229.
† *Life of Alexander Duff,* vol. i. pp. 159, 160.

to almost nothing where the gospel is not found. There appears to be sovereignty in salvation, however much that sovereignty may be opposed. We send the gospel to the heathen, because we believe they are more likely to be saved by the knowledge of it than if they did not possess that knowledge; and, as a matter of fact, thousands heed the gospel call who formerly rejected every other. The numbers of unconverted men outside of Christendom must ever be a tormenting puzzle to Arminianism. Add now to these the fallen angels, who are entirely cut off from salvation, and the puzzle is still more perplexing.

Suppose that twenty persons represent the whole human family from first to last. According to Arminianism, God foreknows, let us say, that fourteen of these will repent and believe as the result of the Spirit's influence: he therefore elects them. The other six will not repent and believe: he therefore condemns them. According to Calvinism, God elects, let us say, fourteen of these persons, and by his Spirit leads them to repent and believe. The other six will not repent and believe: he therefore condemns them. The same number are saved and the same number are lost whichever view is taken. So the one system has no gain over the other in that respect.

Even if we admit that God gives to all men sufficient grace, he yet foreknows that a vast number of men will reject that grace, and be lost for ever as a consequence of that rejection; so we do not find much relief from that theory. We should all know that the chief difficulties touching election are difficulties which belong to the problem of evil. Each thoughtful person will confess that whatever view we take of the divine decrees, there are phases of them which cannot be explained by us. A complete statement has not yet been found. Theology that is studied in heaven will modify many points of the theology which is studied on earth.

The Arminian system is, in the main, pleasant. It seems to us more pleasant than certain facts in the moral government of God—more pleasant than certain teachings of the Bible itself. No person, after looking through it, could be excited to say, "Why doth he yet find fault? For who hath resisted his will?" Rom. ix. 19. The Pauline predestination did prompt such angry questions. The two systems, therefore, must be different.

All Christians, however, when praying to God and praising him, and when stating their experience, confess that it is by free grace alone that they are saved. When the blood-washed throng "shall come from the east and the west, and from the north and the south, and shall sit down in the kingdom of God" (Luke xiii. 29), they will all speak the same language and adore the same Infinite Love. Arminius and Calvin, Wesley and Whitefield, will join hands around the throne.

Election does no injury to those not elected. They receive many favors, and are treated far better than they deserve. If men are lost, God is not the cause of it. If the non-elect will accept of Christ, they will be saved. The door of heaven is shut only against those who refuse to enter. If men prefer not to be religious, they have no reason to find fault with God because he allows them to have their own way.

The thought that a man can do as he pleases if he is only elected is without meaning. The election is to holiness, and no one can infer that he is elected unless he lives a holy life. Both the *means* and the *end* are decreed. If God has purposed that a certain man shall go to Europe, he will not go to Europe unless he enters a ship; and if God has purposed that a certain man shall be saved, he will not be saved unless he fights the good fight of faith.

The practical effects of the doctrine of election are not in the line of evil. The large bodies of men who have believed in it stand favorably as to intelligence and Christian character. Predestination was not the same as "*fate*" to them, and so it had no fatal influence upon their life.

CHAPTER III.

REGENERATION—DIVINE LIFE INTRODUCED INTO THE SOUL BY THE SPIRIT.

I. THAT WHICH IS NOT REGENERATION.

1. To be baptized is not to be regenerated. The Roman Catholic Church, the Greek Church and a party in the Lutheran and Episcopal churches believe in baptismal regeneration. The passage, "Except a man be born of water and of the Spirit, he cannot enter the kingdom of God" (John iii. 5), is viewed as a proof-text for baptismal regeneration. It is not even certain, however, that the words "born of water" refer to baptism: they may simply be a figure for purification. If the language does refer to baptism, it makes known the important truth that a man must *publicly profess* the Christian religion if he would enter the kingdom of God. The outward acknowledgment of the Saviour shows that one has been "born of the Spirit." We read in another passage of "the washing of regeneration and renewing of the Holy Ghost." Tit. iii. 5. The washing is a symbol of regeneration, but not the cause of it. The apostles urged upon men to "*repent*, and be baptized"—*not* that they *should be baptized*, and repent. The thief on the cross was converted, yet not baptized; Simon Magus was baptized, yet not converted. If persons can be regenerated only in baptism, then

all orthodox Friends and all unbaptized infants who die are shut out of heaven. It is a fearful doctrine that our eternal salvation must hang upon the single act of a minister, so that if he does not baptize us we are lost for ever. The mere statement of such a thought is enough to condemn it.

2. Regeneration does not consist in rejecting a religion that is false and believing the religion that is true. A heathen and a Jew may become convinced of the truth of Christianity, the one rejecting heathenism and the other Judaism, but that does not show that the heart is changed. A Unitarian may adopt a Trinitarian form of faith, and a Catholic may approve a sound Protestantism, but this may be nothing more than intellectual assent. Even the man who was a skeptic may become the defender of Christianity, but that does not make him a Christian.

3. There is an experience that precedes the regeneration of adults which may be mistaken for regeneration itself. *a.* Divine truth is realized more clearly than usual. The mind is impressed and solemnized by it. The person is thoughtful. The conscience is sharpened by new light. The claims of God are felt. *b.* There is a sense of danger. The law has been broken. Redemption has been unheeded. The Spirit has been resisted. Probation has been wasted. Eternity is dark. God is displeased. A class of unhappy emotions have taken possession of the soul. *c.* There is a

deep conviction of sin. The man condemns himself. There is no hope. The soul is guilty and lost. *d.* The man prays; the urgency of his condition compels him to pray. He would like others to pray for him. The storm, however, still rages within and without. *e.* A change takes place in the life in certain particulars. A class of sins are set aside. New virtues appear. The Bible is read and the Sabbath is kept. There is a general reformation of character. *f.* The need of redemption springs up in the soul. Help must come from God. If there is no Saviour, there is no heaven.

Now, however favorable all this may be, the new and true life has not yet appeared. There is illumination of the mind, but illumination is not regeneration. If sin were confined to the intellect it would be nothing but *error* or *ignorance.* Sin, however, belongs to the heart and will, and no amount of light can drive it away. Reformation can be seen in the above experience, but reformation is not regeneration. There is an infinite difference between a character that is moral and a character that is evangelical.

II. NATURE OF REGENERATION.

1. Regeneration implies a *radical* change of character. We meet the words "born again," "born of God," "born of the Spirit." To be born is

to begin a new life. The new life of regeneration is spiritual, because the man born of the *Spirit* is put in contrast with the man born of the *flesh*.

2. Regenerating grace is *efficacious*. This means that the grace of God conquers the depravity of man. It is divine Love that conquers, not an iron necessity. Sickness gives way to health, slavery to freedom, sin to holiness.

3. Regenerate character is *permanent* and *governing*. The divine change is in the leading states and tendencies of the soul. There is a supreme and holy principle and a supreme and holy preference. *Light* has come to the *mind*, *life* to the *heart*, *liberty* to the *will*.

4. The change effected in regeneration is *instantaneous*. There can be no progress from a state of depravity to a state of goodness. If the dead are made to live, the life began at a certain moment. There is progress in the knowledge and in the conviction of sin which precede regeneration, but not in regeneration itself.

The state into which men are brought by the new life is the opposite of the state into which they are brought by the fall. First, we have the gift of supernatural grace; secondly, the understanding has a new apprehension of divine things; thirdly, the heart has delight in goodness; fourthly, the will has a holy determination. Thus the entire soul is fundamentally changed. Of course there is no faculty that is absolutely freed from depravity. The chief point is, that the regenerate nature has the mastery.

III. Author of Regeneration.

Regeneration is the act of the Divine Spirit. "God, who is rich in mercy, for his great love wherewith he loved us, even when we were dead in sins, hath quickened us together with Christ" (Eph. ii. 4, 5); "Not by works of righteousness which we have done, but according to his mercy, he saved us, by the washing of regeneration, and renewing of the Holy Ghost." Tit. iii. 5. Divine life must come from the Divine Being. There is no way in which man can *originate* that life. Professor Pope, English Methodist, says: "The Holy Spirit always ends, even as he always begins, the work of goodness in man without human concurrence."* Professor Raymond, American Methodist, says: "Regeneration is a divine work; it is effected immediately by the divine volition operating upon the mind of man; it is without the intervention of second causes; it is of the nature of a miracle."† Our strongest Calvinists do not make the point any sharper than these two writers. John Owen, English Congregationalist, uses this language: "Regeneration consists in a new, spiritual, supernatural, vital principle or habit of grace, infused into the soul, the mind, will and affections by the

---

* *Compendium of Christian Theology*, vol. iii. p. 24.
† *Systematic Theology*, vol. ii. p. 356.

power of the Holy Spirit."* Dr. Charles Hodge, American Presbyterian, says: "According to the evangelical system, regeneration is the act of God's almighty power. Nothing intervenes between his volition that the soul, spiritually dead, should live, and the desired effect."†

If I am asked how the Divine Spirit regenerates the fallen soul, I would answer that I do not know. No man knows. "The wind bloweth where it listeth, and thou hearest the sound thereof, but canst not tell whence it cometh, and whither it goeth: so is every one that is born of the Spirit." John iii. 8. Life in the plant and in the animal is a mystery. Equally mysterious is the commencement of spiritual life in a spiritually dead soul. The regenerative process is back of consciousness. The effects are all that we perceive. It is fair to believe, however, that this regenerative process is in harmony with the constitution of the mind.

Although God is the author of regeneration, he usually works in connection with *preparatory* means. "Of his own will begat he us with the word of truth." James i. 18. We are not accustomed to see men converted in a community or nation where the Bible is not found. The more the means of grace approach the true ideal, the more likely is it that God will bless them. The purer the example of Christians, the purer their teaching, the stronger

---

* *Works*, vol. iii.: "On the Spirit," p. 329.
† *Systematic Theology*, vol. iii. p. 31.

their faith, the more persevering their prayers, the greater is the probability that the Spirit will work in connection with such agencies. The mere fact, then, that regeneration is supernatural gives no encouragement to indolence. We are to appeal to every faculty of the soul, doing our utmost, yet conscious that God only can change the heart.

CHAPTER IV.

SAVING FAITH—THE SOUL LED TO REST ON CHRIST BY THE SPIRIT.

A WORD may be uttered respecting faith and reason. Faith looks to the unseen, and is grounded on divine authority; reason looks to that which is seen, and is its own authority. Sound faith and sound reason never clash. When reason becomes unreasonable it rejects faith, and when faith becomes credulity it rejects reason. God is pure reason; hence if any of his ways appear unreasonable, the fault is ours. If erring man is only humble, he will see that faith begins where reason ends. The greatest philosopher should be the greatest saint. Christianity explains more things, answers more questions and gives more certainty to the troubled mind, than any theory of man. There are phases of truth and life which can be known only by experience. Men will be confused about conversion until they are converted; they will not understand the Saviour until they are saved. While there is a sense in which knowledge must precede love, there is another sense in which love must precede knowledge.

I. That which is not Saving Faith.

1. Merely to believe that the Bible is the *word of God* is not saving faith. This is simply an assent of the understanding. A Christian will believe in the inspiration of Scripture, but to believe in the inspiration of Scripture does not make a man a Christian.

2. Merely to believe that Christ is the *Saviour* will not save the soul. "The devils believe and tremble." We believe that there were such men as Plato and Plutarch, and that there are such cities as London and Paris, although we have never seen the men nor the cities. This belief is founded on testimony, and is called historical faith.

3. I may believe that Christ *died for me*, and yet not be saved.

4. Saving faith does not consist in believing that we are *actually redeemed* by the sufferings and death of Christ. With such a view all that a man has to do is just to believe that he is saved, and he is saved. This is utter trifling.

5. To believe that *my sins are forgiven* is not saving faith. It may be true or it may not be

true that my sins are forgiven. The faith that saves does not centre in that matter, but in Christ.

II. NATURE OF SAVING FAITH.

Saving faith is the *heartfelt acceptance* of the *God-man* as the *only Saviour*. One or all of such words as trust, confidence, reliance, dependence, acceptance may be used to express the act of faith.

Our definition includes the following: *a*. With my *understanding* I believe Christ to be divine and human, and that he made the one atonement for the guilty. I thus do not rest in the highest creature or the holiest man; for to whatever extent such a person might reveal God, he could not redeem mankind. *b*. With my *heart* I feel the need of a divine Saviour. I go to him in penitence; I am supremely attached to him; I adore him because he is infinitely worthy. *c*. With my *will* I accept of him as my only Saviour. I trust my eternally lost soul in his hands, that he may eternally save it; I give myself away to him in a choice that is absolute.

Thus, saving faith takes in the entire mind with its leading faculties. There is the assent of the understanding, the consent of the heart and the resting of the will. A dignity is laid upon faith when it is viewed in this way. There is compass and power to it. Such faith is of necessity a principle of action; holiness will be sure to spring from it. It can no more cease from righteousness than the sun can cease from shining. The apostle Paul, who may be held up as a model Christian, says: "The life which I now live in the flesh I live by the *faith* of the Son of God." Gal. ii. 20. The noted characters mentioned in the Epistle to the Hebrews were all men of faith. Reformers have fought with evil and martyrs have gone to the stake because they believed in Christ. If mere intellectual assent were held up as saving faith, it would be powerless for good; but since the "faith is rooted and grounded in *love*," there is heartfelt obedience. An unholy believer is as great a contradiction as a holy unbeliever.

It may be well to remark that although saving faith centres in the incarnate Redeemer as its chief object, it is not confined to that exalted person. God and his providence, divine truth and the divine law, are all objects of religious faith, and are not less cordially accepted than is Christ himself. Even the faith which is intellectual when exercised with reference to divine realities is spiritualized by the evangelical element.

III. Results of Saving Faith.

1. We are justified by faith. A person is justified when he stands right in the eye of the law. Fallen man is condemned, but by the gospel method of justification he is treated as righteous when he accepts Christ. The righteousness of Christ

is placed to his account as if he had performed it himself. Justification does not make us personally holy: sanctification, however, will be sure to follow in due time. Pardon is not the same thing as justification. When a criminal is pardoned by a human ruler he is delivered from the penalty, but is not viewed as innocent. When the believer is pardoned by the divine Ruler, he is delivered from the penalty and viewed as innocent.

We are said to be justified by faith *alone*, because it is faith which links the soul to the Saviour. We are not justified by faith and works combined, as that would make us, in part, meritorious in our salvation. If it is said that faith itself is a good work, and to that extent we are justified by it, we answer: That to trust in Christ altogether in order to be saved shows that we are absolutely sinful and helpless; and if faith expresses such sinfulness and helplessness, it cannot be viewed as a work of law, having in it the element of legal merit. Faith in a *Saviour* is a qualification made necessary by redemption, and is itself the product of divine grace, and so it cannot be looked upon in the same light as the faith which an angel has in God. Strictly speaking, it is the righteousness of Christ which justifies us, and not our faith.

2. As another result of faith we are adopted into the divine family. "As many as received him, to them gave he power to become the sons of God, even to them that believe on his name." John i. 12.

In this state of sonship the Spirit dwells in us, Christ is our Elder Brother and God is our Father. While upon earth we are trained, chastened, comforted and fitted for heaven. That we are "heirs of God and joint-heirs with Christ" shows the dignity of our position; and so we are prompted to live in a way suitable to it. We possess also the sure title to a heavenly inheritance; and at the last day "we shall be delivered from the bondage of corruption into the glorious liberty of the children of God." Rom. viii. 21.

3. Faith brings us into a most blessed state of union and communion with the Triune God. Believers are "*in* Christ," as if they formed a part of him. They are also "hid with Christ *in* God." Objectively, the Christian is "reconciled to God by the *death* of his Son;" and subjectively, he is united to him by the *life* of that Son. Thus in a double sense "we have peace with God through our Lord Jesus Christ." We are also "*in* the Spirit" and have "joy in the Holy Ghost."

4. There is now the witness of the Spirit. "The Spirit itself beareth witness with our spirit, that we are the children of God." Rom. viii. 16. It is the opinion of good men that the Spirit acts directly on the soul, producing an impression that the person is accepted and saved. The witnessing is of the nature of a new revelation, and the believer knows as certainly that he is a child of God as if he read it in the Bible. It is thought to be reasonable that

"the witnessing act of the Spirit should be as immediate and direct as the justifying or regenerating act."

There is one difficulty in regard to this view—that numbers of pious people know nothing of it by experience. They understand the matter in this way: As they are penitent, believing, loving and determined to live for God, so from *these fruits of the* Spirit they are convinced that they are his followers. Christians are spoken of as "sealed." This shows that the divine image has been stamped upon their heart, by reason of which they have the evidence of sonship, the Spirit meanwhile working through this evidence and making it appear as certain. This way of looking at the subject seems safer than by the theory of immediate suggestion. Satan might take advantage of such a theory, and convince a man that he is a Christian when he is not; but he cannot work with the other view, and generate in the soul holy emotions. Still, if one is sure that the Spirit bears witness directly, be it so; only admit that he also bears witness indirectly.

5. Full assurance is another consequence of saving faith. Faith in Christ and assurance are not the same. I first believe in Christ; then I am assured of my salvation because I do believe. I do not reach heaven because I have a conviction that I am saved, but I reach heaven because I trust in Christ. Many Christians have doubts and fears. These doubts and fears do not arise

from the suspicion that Christianity may be untrue: they arise from the fact that the persons are not sure whether they are children of God. They behold so much evil in their heart, and suffer such mental pain on account of it, that they are perplexed touching their spiritual state. Merely to tell such Christians that salvation is certain, and that they ought to be assured, does not meet their case, because the trouble with them is that they do not fully know that they are Christians, and so they are afraid to make application of the divine promises. It is fair to suppose also that God will not grant the gift of assurance to an inconsistent professor. The perplexity of mind is the result of sin, and the way to banish the perplexity is to banish the sin. " Hereby we do know that we know him, if we keep his commandments." 1 John ii. 3. It is of no use to say to a worldly church-member that he must not look to himself, but to Christ. He has great need to look to himself, and to see whether he is not building on the sand. The course of a class of religionists, in proclaiming their assurance at the very time when their life is proclaiming their selfishness, is purely Antinomian, and is the way to make religion distasteful to men of understanding. We admit that excellent Christians have doubts of their being accepted of God; they do not grasp a finished salvation and rest in Christ: perhaps their mind is clouded by a diseased body, by a native melancholy or by an excess of timidity. The fault with them is not their wayward life. They are the ones who should look to Christ, and not to themselves, resting in him with a trustful faith.

The assurance of hope is a state of high Christian experience, and it can belong only to those who live near to the Saviour. Paul could say, " I *know* whom I have believed, and am persuaded that he is able to keep that which I have committed unto him against that day." 2 Tim. i. 12. The assurance of *hope* and the assurance of *faith* are distinguished from each other. When we are fully assured of the way of salvation through Christ, and of our interest in that salvation, we have the assurance of faith; but when we have a sure expectation of eternal blessedness springing from our faith, we have the assurance of hope. One may have this at the beginning of his religious course, at the middle or toward the end of it, if the conditions are supplied. When once the point is reached, the sky is clear, the sun does not set, the city of God is seen and the soul is at rest.

CHAPTER V.

REPENTANCE—THE TURNING FROM SIN TO HOLINESS BY THE AID OF THE SPIRIT.

I. THAT WHICH IS NOT REPENTANCE.

EVERY part of religion can be counterfeited. There is a spurious faith, penitence, love, hope and obedience. The most of men exercise, at times, what is called *natural* repentance. In this there is the feeling of regret that evil has been done. It was wrong to sin, but the sin was viewed mainly in its human aspects. There may be more or less of shame if the sin has come to the knowledge of other persons. The consequences of wrong-doing affect the mind, rather than the wrong-doing itself. That suffering follows transgression generates fear, and fear prompts to repentance. A fair outward life may now be the result. An awakened conscience, and not a pure heart, has been the chief power at work. Natural repentance is always limited in its range and deficient in its quality. Certain sins are rejected, while other sins are retained. Natural repentance is repentance toward *man*. Evangelical repentance is repentance toward *God*.

II. Nature of Repentance.

"Regeneration is the act of God." Repentance is the act of man—an act put forth under the influence of divine grace and expressing a change of mind. Regeneration is a single act. Repentance is repeated while sin remains. As the results of regeneration are new views of sin and holiness, self and God, Christ and salvation, time and eternity, so repentance connects itself with all these.

If we analyze repentance, it has the following

elements: 1. There is real sorrow because of our sin. The sorrow may be intense or it may be moderate, that depending upon the person's temperament and upon his knowledge in regard to evil. The chief thing is the quality of the sorrow rather than the quantity. 2. There is self-condemnation because sin has been committed. The man upbraids himself, abhors himself, and is ashamed as in the sight of God, apart from what men may think of the evil. 3. There is hatred of sin as sin. It is not that the fruits of sin are bad, or that vice and crime are chiefly detested. Sin itself is hateful, and so it is hated, just as holiness is lovely, and so it is loved. 4. Confession of sin is made to God. While sin is against men, and injures the soul that is guilty of it, there is a feeling that it is mainly against God. There is another feeling, however—that God in Christ is merciful, and that full confession will gain his favor. 5. The man now turns from all sin and makes restitution to those he has defrauded. The simple purpose to amend one's ways is not comprehensive enough to constitute repentance. There must be an unconditional surrender of the soul to God, loving him supremely, having a fixed determination to obey him; and all this connected with a feeling of dependence on Christ. Regeneration, faith and repentance now blend together; and so there is a great voluntary movement of the will that is fixed and continuous. The state of impenitence which formerly held the soul is broken up, and the state of penitence now holds sway. "If any man be in Christ, he is a new creature: old things are passed away; behold, all things are become new." 2 Cor. v. 17.

Christian character is not a single good which can be placed on a level with other good things. It is not to be ranked with fine taste, culture and philanthropy. Religion is not a step toward something higher, that something higher being the chief thing. It is not a means at all: it is the great end of existence. If religion does not reign within making servants of all the faculties of the soul, it is a delusion and a dream.

III. Reasons why Man should Repent.

1. It is a duty. "God commandeth all men everywhere to repent." Acts xvii. 30. Impenitence is rebellion, while penitence shows cordial submission to divine authority. No man has a right to remain a moment away from God. 2. There is no escape from sin unless a man repents. It is certain that if a person will not turn from sin he is held to sin. Repentance is an absolute necessity if one would reach a good life. The requirement is not arbitrary, but reasonable. 3. No man can be forgiven unless he repents. If impenitent men were forgiven, a premium would be offered to sin, and that would be making evil to be good. "Let the wicked forsake his way,

and the unrighteous man his thoughts: and let him return unto the Lord, and he will have mercy upon him; and to our God, for he will abundantly pardon." Isa. lv. 7. 4. Salvation cannot reach a man unless he repents. Salvation is designed to make men holy, but if they will not repent they reject God's remedy for sin. It is either repentance or perdition. "Except ye repent, ye shall all likewise perish." Luke xiii. 5.

IV. Evidence of Repentance.

The spirit of obedience shows that the character is changed. The best evidence that one is a Christian is his Christianity. If parents have entered upon the divine life, the fact will be apparent in the interest felt for their children. They will converse with them on personal piety, and will pray to God in their behalf—things which they never did before. Then the uprising of the missionary spirit, with the willingness to bestow money in order to save distant and unknown men, is a fine evidence of piety. The delight also in those who bear the image of God is a mark of the true religion. "We know that we have passed from death unto life, because we love the brethren." 1 John iii. 14.

The best proof of a holy change is a holy life. Christ says, "He that hath my commandments and keepeth them, he it is that loveth me." John xiv. 21. "Christian practice," remarks President

Edwards, "is plainly spoken of in the word of God as the main evidence of the truth of grace, not only to others, but to men's own consciences. It is not only more spoken of and insisted on than other signs, but in many places where it is spoken of it is represented as the chief of all evidences. . . . Not that there are no other good evidences of a state of grace but this. There may be other exercises of grace besides those efficient exercises which the saints may have in contemplation that may be very satisfying to them, but yet this is the chief and most proper evidence. There may be several good evidences that a tree is a fig tree, but the highest and most proper evidence of it is that it actually *bears figs.*" *

CHAPTER VI.

PRAYER—HOLY DESIRE AWAKENED BY THE SPIRIT.

WE need not be perplexed with the thought as to whether God can answer prayer. That all in the natural and moral world is fixed does not render prayer useless, because means and end are alike decreed, and the natural is made subordinate to the moral. In forming his plan God can easily make prayer a part of it, so that in the outworking of

* *Works*, vol. iii. pp. 213, 216.

this plan rain may fall on a certain day, a sick man may be healed and a bad man may be converted in answer to prayer. Foreordination may include good harvests to certain people, success in trade to certain people, and yet the agency of the persons thus favored could easily have a place in the foreordination.

Besides, by an act of sovereign free will God may modify the course of nature at certain points, just as man modifies it when he forces water up into a reservoir or when he bends the rays of the sun to one side. Surely it is going too far when we are compelled to think of an almighty Being as chained to a system of materialism, having even less power to act upon matter than the creatures he has made.

Objections against prayer from the immutability of law are objections against the existence of God. As their end is atheism, they should be trampled under foot. By "the theory of pre-established harmony" part may fit with part, and the whole system move forward without confusion, there being ample play for matter and mind, ample room for divine and human freedom. It is a remark of John Foster, " that whenever a man prays aright he forgets the philosophy of it, and feels as if his supplications *really would* make a difference in the determination and conduct of the Deity. In this spirit are the prayers recorded in the Bible."*

* *Life and Correspondence*, vol. i. p. 152.

Prayer naturally arises from our sense of weakness and dependence. Then the fact that we are sinners and exposed to manifold evils moves us to pray. Prayer is *desire*. We want strength, forgiveness, reconciliation with God, faith and a pure life, fitness for heaven; and so we put that want into the form of language and tell it to God. All the varied movements of inward piety seem to be of the nature of prayer. Grief because of sin is a sigh for holiness. The feeling of need is a cry for salvation. The feeling of unworthiness proclaims God to be all. Love delights in the Infinite Love, and expresses itself in worship. Faith in Christ makes the worship mediatorial. The consciousness of favors received generates thankfulness. Joy in the Holy Ghost is the renewed spirit ascribing glory to God. The realization of worship is communion with the heavenly Father. The Christian heart is thus a manifold prayer.

I. ONLY TO GOD IS PRAYER TO BE ADDRESSED.

No other person can help us with the kind of help that we need. Angels and glorified spirits can neither hear us nor give what we want. Is it right to pray to Christ? Yes. It would be strange if the person who can save us should not be addressed in prayer. When we sing, "Come, Holy Spirit, heavenly Dove," that is praying to the Spirit; and when we sing, "Jesus, lover of my soul, let me to thy bosom fly," that is praying to Christ. The penitent thief said, "Lord, remember me when thou comest into thy kingdom." Luke xxiii. 42. While it is proper to pray to Christ, the more common method is to pray to God through Christ. He is the Mediator between God and men, and the person who has made atonement for us; so he is both the channel of prayer and the one for whose sake the prayer is answered. "Whatsoever ye shall ask the Father in my name, he will give it you." John xvi. 23.

II. Parts of Prayer.

1. *Adoration.* In this we adore and magnify God. We mention over the divine perfections—as power, holiness, justice and blessedness—expressing our admiration of these. In the book of Psalms the adoration of God is common: "Bless the Lord, O my soul. O Lord my God, thou art very great; thou art clothed with honor and majesty." Ps. civ. 1. The essence of worship centres mainly in adoration. The statements we have respecting the worship of heaven convey this idea: "They rest not day and night, saying, Holy, holy, holy, Lord God Almighty, which was, and is, and is to come." Rev. iv. 8. It is to be feared that the property of adoration is wellnigh gone from our modern Christian worship. The consciousness of self is so extreme that the sense of divine glories does not carry away the soul.

2. *Praise.* Our word "hallelujah" has a He-

brew origin, and is translated in parts of the Bible by the words "Praise the Lord." Rendered literally, it would be "Praise Jah," the word "Jah" being the poetical form for Jehovah. That part of prayer which is of the nature of praise is frequently mentioned in Scripture: "I heard a great voice of much people in heaven, saying, Alleluia; Salvation, and glory, and honor, and power, unto the Lord our God" (Rev. xix. 1); "Praise the Lord, O my soul. While I live will I praise the Lord." Ps. cxlvi. 1, 2. Praise and adoration are linked together, both showing that the soul is enraptured with the excellencies of the Divine Being.

3. *Thanksgiving.* "Oh, give thanks unto the Lord; for he is good: for his mercy endureth for ever." Ps. cxxxvi. 1. All that pertains to life is a matter of thanksgiving. We are living under a redemptive economy, and that economy is a gift. If we have a title to heaven we ought to thank God for his infinite benevolence.

4. *Confession.* We are to realize our sinful state, are to admit that we are guilty, and are to confess to God our sin and guilt, praying to him to forgive us, we heartily repenting. "He that covereth his sins shall not prosper: but whoso confesseth and forsaketh them shall have mercy." Prov. xxviii. 13.

5. *Petition.* We need some good, and we ask God for it. If our heart is indifferent and our

will perverse, we pray that the heart may be interested and the will made obedient. If doubts trouble us and besetting sins carry us away, we pray that they may be removed. We also ask God to bless others. This is an important part of petition. The Christian is an intercessor. He prays that men may be converted, that the people of God may be useful, that nations may dwell in peace and that rulers may govern in wisdom.

III. Kinds of Prayer.

1. The simplest kind of prayer is *ejaculatory*. If we are about to travel by sea or land, we silently pray to God to keep us from danger. Whenever at any moment we feel our ignorance and wickedness we can pray for light and sanctification.

2. *Private Prayer.* Each morning, all alone, before we enter upon our particular business, we pray for grace to enable us to overcome temptation, grace to enable us to show a good example, and that we may live for the glory of God and the good of men. Each evening we pray that the sins of the day may be forgiven, that we may be protected during the night, and that if death comes to us we may be ready. Private prayer should never be omitted. David says, "It is good to show forth thy loving-kindness in the morning, and thy faithfulness every night." Ps. xcii. 2. Again, "Evening, and morning, and at noon, will I pray, and cry aloud: and he shall hear my voice." Ps. iv. 17.

Still further, "Seven times a day do I praise thee, because of thy righteous judgments." Ps. cxix. 164.

3. *Family Prayer.* God is to be recognized and honored in the household. It seems like a species of heathenism to have a family and no fixed worship to begin and end the day. The words are startling: " Pour out thy fury upon the heathen, that know thee not, and upon the families that call not on thy name." Jer. x. 25. Wherever Abraham settled he erected an altar, showing that he could not live without the worship of God. "I query if that beautiful form of prayer which our blessed Lord gave to his followers does not involve an argument in favor of family prayer—nay, of *daily family devotion.* It is worthy of remark that in the sixth chapter of Matthew, after he had directed his disciples with regard to private prayer, he did not stop there. In the seventh verse he begins to use the plural number, and, proceeding to a social act of worship, he refers to the prayers of such as *could* pray *together daily.*" *

4. *Public Prayer.* This brings men together, adds to their religious power, tends to uphold Christianity, becomes a declaration of our faith in God and Christ, and shows that to us religion is supreme. He who disregards public worship is taking sides with the unbeliever. "The Lord loveth the gates of Zion more than all the dwellings of Jacob." Ps. lxxxvii. 2.

* Anderson's *Domestic Constitution*, p. 326.

IV. Prevailing Prayer.

1. If we would prevail with God we must turn from evil. "If I regard iniquity in my heart, the Lord will not hear me." Ps. lxvi. 18. There is not a promise in the Bible that is offered to an impenitent man.

2. If we would have a blessing to come down upon others we must live a consistent life. There is nothing that God loves to honor so much as holiness. "If ye abide in me, and my words abide in you, ye shall ask what ye will, and it shall be done unto you." John xv. 7.

3. Prayer to be acceptable must be offered in faith. "He that cometh to God must believe that he is, and that he is a rewarder of them that diligently seek him." Heb. xi. 6. The prayer of faith must be in harmony with the divine will. "This is the confidence that we have in him, that, if we ask anything according to his will, he heareth us." 1 John v. 14. The Spirit generates the prayer of faith, and such prayer is always answered. A fanatical prayer of faith, the result of a heated fancy, is not answered.

4. In the offering up of supplication I must have a submissive spirit. I am not to dictate to God, as if I beheld the secrets of redemption and knew what should be done in given circumstances. I must be humble and earnest, but not insolent.

5. Acceptable prayer has the characteristic of perseverance. The power to hold on for months

and years is the power that shows character. He that trusts the longest is the strongest. Christ has offered up prayers that will not be answered for ages. God speaks, takes one step—then rests for a thousand years.

CHAPTER VII.

SANCTIFICATION—PROGRESSION IN HOLINESS BY THE POWER OF THE SPIRIT TILL PERFECTION IS REACHED.

JUSTIFICATION is instantaneous, and complete for all believers from the beginning: sanctification is progressive, and so not complete in all believers from the beginning. The former is outward, the latter inward. The one is the judicial and loving *act* of God, and the other is the benevolent *work* of God. In justification we are viewed as standing right in law; in sanctification we keep advancing until we are actually righteous according to the law. In justification we are pardoned and have a title to heaven; in sanctification we are at last purified and fitted for heaven.

To sanctify has two meanings. First, it means to set apart a person or thing to a sacred use. The vessels of the temple were thus sanctified, or set apart to the service of God. Christ says, "I sanctify myself;" that is, I devote myself to the work of redemption. Secondly, to sanctify is to make holy, as in this passage: "The very God of peace sanctify you wholly; and I pray God your whole spirit and soul and body be preserved blameless unto the coming of our Lord Jesus Christ." 1 Thess. v. 23. It is to this latter meaning that we limit ourselves in what follows. The chief end of redemption as related to the Christian is the production of holiness, and the chief end of the Christian is to reach holiness through that redemption.

I. GOD THE EFFICIENT AGENT IN SANCTIFICATION.

"And I will give them one heart, and I will put a new spirit within you; and I will take the stony heart out of their flesh, and will give them a heart of flesh: that they may walk in my statutes, and keep mine ordinances, and do them" (Ezek. xi. 19, 20); "I have planted, Apollos watered; but God gave the increase. So then, neither is he that planteth anything, neither he that watereth; but God that giveth the increase." 1 Cor. iii. 6, 7. There is not a particle of holiness in the world but that can be traced to a supernatural origin. Of course there is a sense in which the work of sanctification may be called divine-human. The Christian has in him a new nature, and that new nature co-operates with the Spirit. We work out our salvation because God works in us.

II. Means of Sanctification.

1. As Scripture reveals to us the leading thoughts relating to God and man, the divine law and the eternal state, the way of salvation and the conditions by which it becomes ours, so Scripture is the chief instrumentality in the development of holiness. "Sanctify them through thy truth: thy word is truth." John xvii. 17. Sometimes a single sentence of the Bible will inspire the whole soul, moving it forward in deeds of purity. Divine truth, with its authority, certainty, and complete adaptation to the wants of man, is used by the Spirit as the most suitable means in the work of sanctification.

2. Then we have the ordinances of divine worship. These are of like character and tendency with the truth of God. The preaching, prayer, praise and the sacraments are all means of grace to the mind that is obedient. Let persons fail in their attendance upon public worship, and their decline in piety is certain. One of the surest ways to undermine the Christian religion is to set light by the Sabbath and the sanctuary.

3. The afflictions of life have a sanctifying influence. "No chastening for the present seemeth to be joyous, but grievous: nevertheless, afterward it yieldeth the peaceable fruit of righteousness unto them which are exercised thereby." Heb. xii. 11. The mind is subdued and softened under affliction; the attractions of earth lose their power; the eye

is fixed on heaven; the soul is drawn toward God; character is felt to be of greater value than all things else.

4. Witnessing a holy example leads to holiness. Reading the biographies of saintly men makes us wiser and better. The life of Christ, however, has power above every other life. His loveliness makes us to see our deformity, causing us to long to be like him. We sigh as he passes before us, as if we were praying in the depths of our being for his aid, feeling that we shall never become well till his life has become ours. In the darkness he is the light of our way, and at the end of our path he is heaven. "We all, with open face beholding as in a glass the glory of the Lord, are changed into the same image from glory to glory, even as by the Spirit of the Lord." 2 Cor. iii. 18.

III. SANCTIFICATON THROUGH CONFLICT.

1. By struggling against sinful tendencies. In conversion the work of holiness is only begun. A corrupt nature and evil habits are to be destroyed. A cross meets the soul at the beginning, and meets it all the way through life. The cross, however, is not peculiar to Christianity. It connects itself with whatsoever is valuable in time. To reach mental power or proficiency in any calling is not possible without the cross. There is a cross in every climate and every season, in the land and in the sea, in the air and in the light,

in the body and in the soul, in all governments and all relations. Being imperfect, we are under discipline; so the Christian must battle with evil. If he fights not, he wins not. In proportion as we weaken evil habits we strengthen good habits. If one will note down on paper his sinful tendencies, he will see the work to be done, and will be startled at the depravity which clings to the soul. There is pride, envy, jealousy, a movement of revenge, impatience, evil-speaking, selfishness, a degree of untruthfulness, the unforgiving spirit, worldly-mindedness, frivolity, uncharitableness, anger, moroseness, sins of the flesh in thought or act, the tendency to forget God. Then all the sins of omission,—what a list they would make! It is no easy work to set the soul right.

2. Natural tendencies need to be regulated. Certain souls are impetuous and rash; others are sluggish and passive—the one class needing to be checked, the other excited. Then we have the happiness instinct, seeking to turn virtue into enjoyment; the love of fame and the love of power; the possessory principle and self-love: to shape and turn these will demand effort. Our greatest powers are our greatest danger. The soul that can be eternally saved is the soul that can be eternally lost. It is a fearful thing to be a man.

3. Certain tendencies of the age need to be **resisted**. There is a materialistic drift which is

destructive of all good, and it must be opposed. There is a rationalistic tendency which is irrational; it must be met by the authority of God. The attempt to soften the severe aspects of divine truth and the Divine Being is not to be countenanced. Sin and Justice are stern realities, even though Mercy has in her hand the cup of salvation.

IV. Sanctification gained by Direct Efforts.

There are five states of mind in regenerate man which form the groundwork of sanctification.

First, there is a penitential state; secondly, a state which is of the essence of prayer; thirdly, a state of faith; fourthly, a state of love; fifthly, a state of obedience.

The Christian soul is never without any one of these spiritual states. If they are properly developed they will end in perfection. Cultivating holy frames of mind is the surest and quickest way of attaining holiness. Acts will come forth like gold coin from the mint when the frames of mind are pure and fervent. Of course we must attend to individual duties, and must see that they appear at the right time and have the exact weight which the law of God requires. We are to aim at singleness of holy quality in actions—that is, that they be not mixed with secondary or sinful motives. Every Christian grace also must beautify the soul as with the gems of heaven. There must be humility, submission, tenderness, long-suffering, self-control, benevolence, meekness, heavenly-mindedness. The positive virtues must all come forth like stars. We are not to be satisfied with *supreme* love to God, thinking that that is the fulfilling of the law. When love has the governing power it is called supreme. It must go so far, however, as to *fill* the soul; then it will be the love of *totality*, and not mere supremacy. Sanctification must spread over all the faculties; the very essence of the mind must be holiness.

V. Is Sinless Perfection attainable in the Present Life.

The majority of Christians believe that no sinless man has appeared since the fall of Adam except "the man Christ Jesus." Persons noted for piety are conscious of indwelling sin. The Bible addresses those who are sinful. The exhortations, commands and warnings are for imperfect men. The prayers and promises are for men struggling to be holy. "We have an advocate with the Father" because we sin. The entire apparatus of salvation is for sinners. This of course does not imply that men are excusable when they come short of perfection, or that they are necessitated to sin. Every human being is under obligation to be perfectly holy, but the life does not correspond with the obligation. That it is our duty to keep God's law is no evidence that some do keep it.

Certain pious men affirm that entire sanctification is reached by an instantaneous act of faith. We call in question this affirmation. It is easy to be mistaken in regard to a matter that has so many particulars. Christians may attain to a state of assurance by an act of faith, and, being enraptured with the peace and joy which flow from this assurance, they may imagine it to be sanctification itself when it is not. The work of sanctification is progressive as far as we know. Men must understand the entire range of duty before they can do it; and to gain such knowledge requires time. We are to "grow in grace, and in the knowledge of our Lord and Saviour Jesus Christ" (2 Pet. iii. 18); "The path of the just is as the shining light, that shineth more and more unto the perfect day." Prov. iv. 18. We admit that at the moment of death the believer is perfected in holiness by an instantaneous act of the Divine Spirit, but why he should wait till that particular time before he effects a complete cure in souls we do not know. Our view of God's grace leads us to see divine sovereignty in sanctification as well as in regeneration.

CHAPTER VIII.

PERSEVERANCE OF THE SAINTS—THE SPIRIT NEVER LEAVES THE CHILDREN OF GOD.

Two kinds of passages are addressed to Christians in the Bible—one kind seeming to intimate that they may be lost, and the other that they will be saved. Take these verses as samples: "We ought to give the more earnest heed to the things which we have heard, lest at any time we should let them slip" (Heb. ii. 1); "My sheep hear my voice, and I know them, and they follow me: and I give unto them eternal life; and they shall never perish, neither shall any man pluck them out of my hand." John x. 27, 28. The difference in these two passages is a difference of standpoint. The first is only seemingly against the perseverance of the saints; the second is directly in favor of that perseverance. Certain admissions, however, may be made.

1. The way to heaven is one of *danger*. If the Christian has holiness in his heart, he has also sin; and that sin he must fight against. "The world, the flesh and the devil" are striving to ruin him: he must overcome these. The passage sounds in his ear: "He that endureth to the end shall be saved." Matt. x. 22. It is only with the utmost difficulty that one can reach heaven. The incitements and warnings, therefore, instead of showing

that the Christian may be lost, are the means by which he is saved. Paul stated to those in the vessel with him that there should be no loss of any man's life, but when he saw the sailors attempting to escape, he said, "Except these abide in the ship, ye cannot be saved." Acts xxvii. 31. Certain things must be done if all were to reach the land in safety.

Although eternal life is sure to the Christian, he must so run that he shall obtain it.

When the Bible announces that a man is justified by faith, the understanding is that the faith necessitates good works. Although the decree of election makes it certain that the people of God shall be saved, they do not ground their salvation on that decree, as they have no means of knowing it; but they ground it on their faith in Christ; and in order to be sure in the matter, they judge of the soundness of their faith by the soundness of their life. The pious man feels that he must use every power of his mind in the service of Christ, just as if his soul's salvation depended upon his own efforts. No religious person will take advantage of any phase of truth for the purpose of encouraging laxity in life. The idea of a Christian is that of one who is struggling to be perfectly holy. No one can embrace sin and embrace the Saviour at the same time.

2. The Christian *would certainly fall away and be lost for ever* if God were to leave him to himself.

Let the Divine Spirit retire from the earth, and all would sink to ruin. The strongly Calvinistic "Canons of Dort" say plainly that "by reason of the remains of indwelling sin, and the temptations of sin and of the world, those who are converted could not persevere in a state of grace if left to themselves."* This, however, is merely hypothetical. "God hath not cast away his people which he foreknew." Rom. xi. 2.

3. The disciple of Christ has *natural power* to commit any sin. The Christian father has power to kill his entire family as truly as godless persons have, but he has no heart to do such things. It is morally impossible for him to act in the way supposed. "Whosoever is born of God doth not commit sin; for his seed remaineth in him: and he cannot sin, because he is born of God." 1 John iii. 9.

4. Persons who to *all appearance* were Christians have at last lost their souls. As far as these individuals were known by others—and, it may be, by themselves—they were thought of as converted, and yet they were not converted. They were simply the stony-ground hearers who appeared well for a time. When temptations came their surface piety fell to pieces. Many such persons have been in the Church, and they are cited as proofs of falling from grace. We cannot accept such evidence. "They went out from us, but

---

* Schaff, *Creeds of Christendom*, vol. i. p. 523.

they were not of us; for if they had been of us, they would no doubt have continued with us." 1 John ii. 19.

We admit that the regenerate sometimes commit great sin, but it is certain that they will confess and forsake their sin. The heartfelt penitence of David and of Peter is evidence that the principle of grace was not lost in these men. The instant they saw their wickedness they turned to God. It is in this readiness to own their guilt that we behold the outworking of a nature that is still regenerate. Unconverted men may commit the same sins as the king of Israel and the apostle of Christ, but they have no such spirit of penitence as they manifested. If a professed Christian fall into evil, and continue in it in spite of all warnings to the contrary, assuredly he was never born of the Spirit. The determination to hold on to *one sin* proves the person a hypocrite.

We meet, however, with this objection: "As Adam and the angels fell, so Christians may be expected to fall. If perfectly holy beings sinned and lost everything, how much more may the partially sanctified sin and lose everything!" At first sight the argument is plausible, but it proves too much. It forces us to believe that not a single child of God will reach heaven, because, if the argument is sound, since perfect creatures lost all, the probabilities are increased a thousand-fold that imperfect creatures will lose all. If salvation by grace is not different, in some new and high sense, from salvation by law, then we are all doomed.

Let what follows be noted.

When a holy being sins for the *first time* he loses *all goodness.* The first sin affects the entire spiritual nature; there is nothing but total depravity; the fallen creature will sin for ever. Now, when a regenerate man sins the first time after his conversion, he does not lose all goodness. If he did lose all goodness by simply committing one sin, then after that one sin he could not perform a single holy act, because there is no holy disposition in the soul to lead in that direction. It is a fact, however, that the holy disposition is not lost by the first sin committed after conversion. Here, then, is a point that we ought to look at. Why should the holy nature of a Christian *remain* when he falls, while the holy nature of Adam and the angels *did not remain* when they fell? It is evident that creatures are different as to their character under the remedial influence of mercy from creatures under the retributive influence of law.

But if the holy disposition of the Christian is not lost by the commission of the first sin after regeneration, how is it by the commission of the second, third or fourth sin? We know that it is not lost even then. The best of men sin every day, and yet the principle of regeneration abides. Adam and the angels were lost by one sin, but pious men are not lost by many sins. If the latter were in the same hopeless state as the former, they would need to be regenerated after the commission of each sin, and so they would be converted hundreds of times during a year. One regeneration, however, is all that is wanted.

We have this additional thought: The strength of the divine principle is seen, not simply from the fact that it remains after all the assaults of sin and temptation, but from this other fact, that it positively overcomes sin and temptation and extends the area of goodness. When this divine principle is introduced into the heart it does not find there a righteousness ready to receive it. A vast number of acts of holiness, therefore, have to be performed for the first time. Sins that have been usually committed are now set aside, and deeds of love take their place. Evil habits also give way before those that are good. It is clear that holiness is no mere exotic from a tropical clime, which must wither the moment sin strikes it. Like the symbolic tree of life which grows in heaven, it yields its fruit every month, and its leaves are for the healing of the nations.

There is no way of accounting for the stability of a holy disposition in the regenerate except by the special intervention of God. Since the Divine Spirit used great effort to lead a man to Christ, holding on to him though resisted at every step, and finally overcoming his opposition by the omnipotency of love, there is no reason why he should leave him at the point of conversion. As repentance and faith are the gifts of God, so perseverance and purity are his gifts. He begins, carries forward and finishes the work of grace in the soul. "Whom he did predestinate, them he also called: and whom he called, them he also justified: and whom he justified, them he also glorified. What shall we then say to these things? If God be for us, who can be against us?" Rom. viii. 30, 31. One step leads to the other. Even in the first acceptance of Christ there is an element of finality. As all men fell by the first Adam, so all believers stand secure in the second Adam. If eternal salvation rests ultimately with the Christian, he cannot be sure but that he will be lost. "He is kept, however, by the power of God through faith unto salvation." 1 Pet. i. 5.

Dr. Pope, the distinguished Methodist theologian, is willing to go as far as this: "However viewed, the grace of Christ toward his own, and the power of the Holy Spirit within them, go far to secure absolutely the final salvation of the regenerate. The surpassing and unlimited love of the Redeemer, the reluctance of the Spirit to forsake the work of his hands, the growing blessedness of true religion, the might of intercessory prayer both divine and human, the feebleness of the Lord's enemies in comparison of his lightest influence,—all conspire to show that the utter relapse and final ruin of a regenerate soul is a *hard possibility*." *

* *Compendium of Theology*, vol. iii. p. 135.

PART V.

DOCTRINE CONCERNING THE LAST THINGS.

CHAPTER I.

STATE OF SOULS BETWEEN DEATH AND THE RESURRECTION.

DOES the soul sleep after death? The following passages are quoted as proof: "Now shall I sleep in the dust" (Job vii. 21); "Lighten mine eyes, lest I sleep the sleep of death" (Ps. xiii. 3); "Many of them that sleep in the dust of the earth shall awake" (Dan. xii. 2); "Our friend Lazarus sleepeth" (John xi. 11); "Them which sleep in Jesus will God bring with him." 1 Thess. iv. 14. The word "sleep" in these verses is taken *literally*, whereas the majority of readers, who understand the common usage of language, take it *figuratively*. When we sing the hymn, "Asleep in Jesus, blessed sleep," we never imagine that the person who is dead is really asleep. Death is frightful to the most of men, and the tendency is to use figurative expressions when speaking of it. Hence persons prefer to say that they *lost* a friend, rather than to say that the friend is *dead*. We speak also of the *departed*. This is scriptural. Paul says, "The time of my *departure* is at hand." 2 Tim. iv. 6. Moses and Elias spake of Christ's "decease;" that is, of his *departure*—in Greek *exodon*, exodus. If we are gazing at one who has just ceased to breathe, we say, "He is *gone;*" perhaps adding the words, "gone to his long *home.*" All this is natural, and there is no need of misunderstanding such a common style of language. To believe that all the dead of past generations are in a state of unconsciousness is a dismal thought. Such a blank existence for hundreds or thousands of years, even of the wisest and best of men, is contrary to the analogy of nature.

There is another view which has been forcing itself into notice by a class of Second Adventists— namely, this: that man has no soul separate from the body; he is *wholly material.* To be made in the image of God is to be "made in his *external* likeness." The Divine Being has a "personal form," has eyes and ears, hands and feet. The word "spirit" means *wind,* so man is material; and God being a spirit, he also is material. When it is said, "The Lord God formed man of the *dust of the ground*" (Gen. ii. 7), that is understood to teach that man is nothing but matter. The penalty of the law is temporal death. When men are dead they are out of existence, annihilated. With such a view there is no sleep of the soul; there is no immaterial soul that can sleep. Thus the rank materialism of the unbeliever is presented to us as if it were the teaching of Scripture. Vogt, that prince of skeptics, says: "The existence of a soul which uses the brain as an instrument with which to work as it pleases is utter nonsense. Physiology distinctly and categorically pronounces against any individual immortality, and against all ideas which are connected with the figment of a separate existence of the soul."* It is remarkable that professedly religious men should join hands with those who reject all religion. With such a theory there is no need of any atonement, because each man satisfies the law by suffering the penalty of death. In fact, there is no sin which calls for an atonement, because if man is simply material sin is nothing but disease, and what he needs is a physician, not a Saviour. More than this, the theory destroys the very existence of God, because if the Deity is material he is limited, is not self-sufficient, is not free.

"The word *ruah* occurs three hundred and seventy-eight times in the Hebrew Scriptures of the Old Testament, and, after carefully examining all these passages in their connections, we are prepared to assert that it is most commonly to be rendered either *wind* or *spirit.*" . . . "The Hebrew word *nephesh* occurs five hundred and seventy-four times in the Old-Testament books, and it should be trans-

* Quoted in Christlieb's *Modern Doubt*, p. 146.

lated *breath* once; *perfume* once: *creature* eighteen times; *person* two hundred and one times; *body* twenty-six times; *life* one hundred and seventy-five times; *vital principle* sixty-one times; *mind* two hundred and eight times; *feeling* fifty-three times; *self* ten times." * That *nephesh* means the immaterial soul can be seen by a glance at this passage: "Shall I give my first-born for my transgression, the fruit of my body for the sin of my soul?" Mic. vi. 7. Here it is put in contrast with the body.

The true view of the state of the soul after death is this: As there are two classes of men, the good and the bad, so there are two places, one of blessedness and one of misery, to which souls go as character determines. Paul says: "We are confident, and willing rather to be absent from the body, and to be present with the Lord." 2 Cor. v. 8. To be present with the Lord can mean nothing less than to be in heaven. "I am in a strait betwixt two, having a desire to depart, and to be with Christ; which is far better." Eph. i. 23. To be with Christ cannot mean to be asleep or to be out of existence. When the godly Stephen prayed, "Lord Jesus, receive my spirit" (Acts vii. 29), the fair inference is that his spirit went to Jesus. The Saviour said to the penitent robber, "To-day shalt thou be with me in paradise." Luke xxiii. 43.

* Rev. William H. Cobb, *Biblioth. Sacra*, vol xxxvii. pp. 136, 138.

Paradise must have the same meaning as heaven, for Paul calls it the third heaven, where he "heard things that were unutterable." 2 Cor. xii. 4. The third heaven was understood by the Jews to be the dwelling-place of God. The reward granted to the victorious Christian is that he will "eat of the tree of life, which is in the midst of the paradise of God." Rev. ii. 7. Paradise does not seem to be any middle place where the righteous dwell till the morning of the resurrection. The Epistle to the Hebrews states that in the heavenly Jerusalem are found " an innumerable company of angels," " God the Judge of all," " the spirits of just men made perfect, and Jesus the mediator of the new covenant." Heb. xii. 22–24. Then we have that striking passage in the book of Revelation : " I saw under the altar the souls of them that were slain for the word of God, and for the testimony which they held: and they cried with a loud voice, saying, How long, O Lord, holy and true, dost thou not judge and avenge our blood on them that dwell on the earth ?" Rev. vi. 9, 10. " Here are seen *under* the altar—*i. e.* at the foot of it—in imploring attitude, the souls of men already slain for their fidelity to Christ and his gospel. It seemed to them that truth was suffering, that Christ's kingdom was going down, that justice was outraged, by the longer permission of such horrible persecutions, and even by the delay of righteous retribution upon their murderers. God heard their cry and answered."* That beautiful verse which is often used at funerals is full of heavenly meaning: "Blessed are the dead which die in the Lord from henceforth: Yea, saith the Spirit, that they may rest from their labors; and their works do follow them." Rev. xiv. 13. That is, from the moment of death they are in a state of blessedness. Turning now to the parable of the Rich Man and Lazarus, we learn that the rich man after death was in torment, while Lazarus was in the bosom of Abraham.

The Irish Articles of Religion (A. D. 1615) have these words: "After this life is ended the souls of God's children be presently received into heaven, there to enjoy unspeakable comforts; the souls of the wicked are cast into hell, there to endure eternal torments."† The Westminster Confession of Faith (A. D. 1647) has a fuller statement: "The bodies of men, after death, return to dust, and see corruption; but their souls (which neither die nor sleep), having an immortal subsistence, immediately return to God who gave them. The souls of the righteous, being then made perfect in holiness, are received into the highest heavens, where they behold the face of God in light and glory, waiting for the full redemption of their bodies: and the souls of the wicked are cast into hell, where they remain in torments and utter darkness, reserved

---

* Cowles, *Notes on the Book of Revelation*, p. 101.
† Schaff, *Creeds of Christendom*, vol. iii. p. 543.

to the judgment of the great day. Besides these two places for souls separated from their bodies, the Scripture acknowledgeth none."*

There is danger in taking up with a middle place where souls are to remain till the resurrection. Once advocate the notion that there is an intermediate place, which is neither heaven nor hell, and it will not be long before men will make it a training-school where souls are fitted for the skies, made ready for heaven's blessedness.

Will there be a probation after death for those persons who were destitute of the knowledge of Christ in the present life? No. The Bible makes it plain that salvation is confined to the *earth* and *time*. There is not an instance in Scripture of a man's repenting in perdition. "Their worm dieth not, and the fire is not quenched" (Mark ix. 44); "Whatsoever thy hand findeth to do, do it with thy might; for there is no work, nor device, nor knowledge, nor wisdom, in the grave, whither thou goest" (Eccles. ix. 10); "As many as have sinned without law shall also perish without law." Rom. ii. 12. The heathen know vastly more than they practice. They are condemned by their own conscience, and why should they not be condemned by a holy and just God? They are spoken of as "guilty" and as "without excuse." It is not so much the want of knowledge that condemns men as it is the want of a right state of mind. If an

* Schaff, *Creeds of Christendom*, vol. iii. p. 670.

African or a Hindoo has "a broken and a contrite heart, God will not despise" him.

No argument for a future probation can be based on the difficult passage where it is stated that Christ "went and preached unto the spirits in prison." 1 Pet. iii. 19. We know that the Saviour after his death went to "paradise," and not to the place of the lost. Besides, there is an *impassable gulf* which separates the good from the bad, thus leaving no way by which the knowledge of salvation can be conveyed to the wicked. As far as the ungodly are concerned who were swept away by the Flood, they are spoken of as "reserved unto the day of *judgment* to be *punished*" (2 Pet. ii. 9), showing that for them there is no hope.

CHAPTER II.

THE MILLENNIUM.

The word "millennium" has reference to the thousand years of exalted life mentioned in the twentieth chapter of the Revelation. It was thought by some in the early Church that these thousand years began with Christ and would close with the tenth century, the end of the world being then expected. This is one extreme. Another extreme is to place the millennium "*after the judgment*—to hold that after the Bridegroom comes and the beloved city is completed Christ shall move his saints home, and live and reign with them in the new heaven and new earth."*

The more common view of the Church is that the millennium refers to a time in the future when the Christian religion shall have the ascendency in all countries. As the exalted Christian dwells for a season in the "Land Beulah" before the journey ends, so the exalted Church dwells for a season in the Land Beulah before the present dispensation closes.

Martensen throws out a speculation of this character: "As the millennial reign is an actual prophecy of the glory of perfection, nature also will exhibit prophetic indications, anticipating its future glorification; and though Christ will not be raised up in a literal and sensitive manner to his kingly dominion, yet his presence will not be merely spiritual; visible manifestations of Christ will, during this period, be granted to the faithful, like those to the disciples after the resurrection. According to this view, the thousand years' reign would correspond with the interval of forty days between the resurrection and the ascension—an interval which implies the transition from earthly existence to heavenly glory." †

The Scriptures point out with fullness of statement the blessed age. That blessed age is to us

---

* Miller's *Lectures on the Second Coming of Christ*, p. 236.
† *Christian Dogmatics*, p. 471.

the chief thing, and not the technical number, a thousand years. Whether the thousand years are to be understood literally or as expressive of an indefinite number we need not be anxious to inquire. Persons may find themselves *in* the millennium without knowing when it *began,* and persons may find themselves *out* of the millennium without knowing when it *ended.*

1. It is remarkable that it is the prophets of the *Jewish dispensation* who speak of a time when all nations shall be blessed.* That the men were Jews, natives of a small country, and their religion chiefly confined to that country, makes it strange that they should mark out so distinctly a time when both Jews and Gentiles would be happy in the Lord. Then, too, what is noteworthy, they were generally in the midst of darkness and discouragement when they penned the words relating to the bright future. If the logic of surrounding events had influenced them, they would have thought of ruin.

2. It is equally strange that the descriptions of the blessed age should be found in the *Old Testament,* and not in the *New.* We should have thought that the New Testament would be the book that would be radiant with such descriptions. The Christian dispensation, with its one atonement, one religion for all mankind and one mission of the Spirit, is the final dispensation. The canon of

* I am indebted to Isaac Taylor for many of the thoughts of this chapter.

Scripture is also closed with the New Testament. Surely, then, the bright revelations of the period of universal good shall be found there. Not so. Our skill in thinking what the Bible should be is no better than our skill in thinking what the creation should be.

3. The prophetic utterances respecting the time we call the millennium relate chiefly to *collections of men*. We behold nations, the world, in a state of life. "The earth shall be full of the knowledge of the Lord, as the waters cover the sea." Isa. xi. 9. Here the people are massed together, the ocean being the symbol. The national idea is brought out in this passage: "All kings shall fall down before him: all nations shall serve him." Ps. lxxii. 11. The New Testament is more individual than the Old. Our personality is struck by the words, "Repent, every one of you."

4. When the prophets speak of the Church of the future they point to *time* and this *earth*, and not to *eternity* and *heaven*. The New Testament is remarkable for its vast sweep of thought: we are made to think of the totality of existence. "We look not at the things which are seen, but at the things which are not seen: for the things which are seen are temporal; but the things which are not seen are eternal." 2 Cor. iv. 18. The Old Testament is singular in its long lines of earthly vision. This arose in part from the many temporal rewards and punishments which came to the Jews. Still,

the Old Testament has its passages relating to eternity and heaven: "I shall be satisfied, when I awake, with thy likeness" (Ps. xvii. 15); "They that be wise shall shine as the brightness of the firmament; and they that turn many to righteousness, as the stars for ever and ever." Dan. xii. 3.

5. The modern watchword of *universal brotherhood* is a biblical thought. "Humanity," says Max Müller, "is a word which you look for in vain in Plato or Aristotle; the idea of mankind as one family, as the children of one God, is an idea of Christian growth; and the science of mankind and of the languages of mankind is a science which, without Christianity, would never have sprung into life. When people had been taught to look upon all men as brethren, then, and then only, did the variety of human speech present itself as a problem that called for a solution in the eyes of thoughtful observers; and I therefore date the real beginning of the science of language from the first day of Pentecost."*

6. During the millennium *righteousness shall generally prevail.* "From the rising of the sun even unto the going down of the same, my name shall be great among the Gentiles; and in every place incense shall be offered unto my name, and a pure offering: for my name shall be great among the heathen, saith the Lord of hosts" (Mal. i. 11); "Blindness in part is happened to Israel, until the

* *Science of Language*, p. 128.

fullness of the Gentiles be come in. And so all Israel shall be saved." Rom. xi. 25, 26. "The 'fullness' of the Gentiles constitutes a definite but immense number whom God foreknew, called and justified in the manner previously described by the apostle. St. Paul here asserts the Christianization of the globe prior to the Christianization of the Jews. In neither case, however, is it necessary to suppose the regeneration of every individual without exception. Yet the terms *fullness* and *all*, applied to the elect, imply that the non-elect will be comparatively few."* That the world is to be converted may look to the skeptical mind as a pleasant dream. The Church of God, however, goes forward in its work of evangelization, believing that the grain of mustard-seed is to become a great tree. When all things are fully prepared there will doubtless be unusual manifestations of the Divine Spirit, by which means millions will come to Christ at once. If three thousand persons were converted by the one sermon of Peter, what may we not expect when the gospel is preached in its purity and power all over the earth? "The Spirit is to be poured out upon all flesh" in a way that we have never seen. False systems will assuredly break up when the millennium appears, and persons will outwardly, if not inwardly, fall in with the religion of Christ. Although Christians at that time will not be sinless,

* Shedd, *Commentary on Romans*, p. 347.

they will possess a high degree of holiness; and so, as they live near to God, they will be instrumental in turning many to righteousness. The very conversion of the Jews will react upon the Gentiles, and a great wealth of spiritual life will be the result.

7. The time will be one of great *happiness.* "The ransomed of the Lord shall return, and come to Zion with songs and everlasting joy upon their heads; they shall obtain joy and gladness, and sorrow and sighing shall flee away." Isa. xxxv. 10. How soft and beautiful is such language! The people seem to "summer in bliss upon the hills of God." Joy as a queen sits enthroned in the hearts of men, and the Sabbath of souls has come with its smile. Each one seems to be sitting by a lake where all is peace, sitting in an arbor where all is love, or pleasantly walking through the gardens and groves of the saved—walking amidst the radiance and glory of the eternal morning. The happiness of those years is connected with *God.* "The sun shall be no more thy light by day; neither for brightness shall the moon give light unto thee: but the Lord shall be unto thee an everlasting light, and thy God thy glory." Isa. lx. 19. One listens to such language as he listens to music at night—attentive to the sound and wishing that it may be continued.

8. A *golden age* is the prophetic idea of that

future time. The joyous days when Adam and Eve were in Paradise appear to be restored. Innocence and love, simplicity and peace, mark the hours. There is nothing that will harm. The very beasts lose their wildness. "The wolf shall dwell with the lamb, and the leopard shall lie down with the kid; and the calf and the young lion and the fatling together; and a little child shall lead them." Isa. xi. 6. That there is poetry about such pictures is to be admitted. There is an attempt to represent the ideal. The mind is struggling to shape to itself a golden age, and consequently nature is made to yield up its treasures in order to give form to the conception. The luminaries of heaven act a part; the hills sing with gladness; the trees clap their hands. The earth is to be a glorious earth, and all things are to be gilded with the joys of the Lord.

At the end of the thousand years there is to be an outbreak of evil. "Satan shall be loosed out of his prison, and shall go out to deceive the nations which are in the four quarters of the earth, Gog and Magog, to gather them together to battle: the number of whom is as the sand of the sea. And they went up on the breadth of the earth, and compassed the camp of the saints about, and the beloved city: and fire came down from God out of heaven, and devoured them." Rev. xx. 7-9. Hardened men, leagued with Satan and led on by him, are to assail the good. This is to be the last struggle—fierce, but short. At the very time when the wicked are heated and hurried forward with malice they are struck down by the judgments of God. Then comes the end here: the endless is in the great Hereafter.

CHAPTER III.

THE SECOND COMING OF CHRIST.

There are comings of Christ which are not visible. "When they persecute you in this city, flee ye into another: for verily I say unto you, Ye shall not have gone over the cities of Israel, till the Son of man be come" (Matt. x. 23); "There be some standing here, which shall not taste of death, till they see the Son of man coming in his kingdom." Matt. xvi. 28. These verses cannot apply to the second coming of Christ. Whether they point to a special judgment or mercy is of no great importance. History, at any rate, has its comings of Christ in both judgment and mercy, and these are typical of the final advent of the Son of God.

Christ is to come in great glory, with the collective hosts of heaven around him. Thus the second advent will be in marked contrast with the first, one being noted for its servant-like state and circumstances, and the other for its royalty and splendor.

Attempts have been made to fix the time when

Christ shall come, but all such attempts have failed. It is the fact that he *will come* we are to look at, and not the year, month or week. "Of that day and that hour knoweth no man, no, not the angels which are in heaven, neither the Son, but the Father." Mark xiii. 32. Such a passage ought to check all speculations touching the time of the second advent. " While it is right and proper for Christians in this age of the world to observe the signs of the times, and endeavor to gird up their loins and watch for the coming of the Lord, it is an evidence of shallowness and cause of much evil-speaking when at every political event, supposed to be very great because very near the observer, they give forth a new calculation to fix the date when the dispensation will come to a close. Unbelievers are indeed ready to scoff at the purest profession of faith in God, but disciples should beware lest they give adversaries occasion to repeat their sneers. The prophecies of Scripture reveal the coming event, and keep it before us like a star in the firmament, but they do not inform us how near it is." It may seem to manifest strong faith for a man to say he does not expect to die, but expects to live till Christ comes; and yet it is a fair question whether it would not show as much piety to be more modest, especially since so many enthusiastic persons have been compelled to die without seeing their Lord.

Eager and penetrating men tell us that the present decline in religion is evidence that Christ is about to come. But we may question the assertion on which their argument stands. Christianity in England, Germany and America during the last century was in a worse state than it is at present. However imperfect religion may be (and it is imperfect), there is more of it just now than in any age of the past. If one wants to see decline in religion, why not look at the Dark Ages? Yet Christ did not appear then—did not appear even though expectant men thought he would. In fact, every Christian century has had its season of decay. Even the first age, with its personal Saviour, inspired apostles and array of miracles, had an eclipse of the faith. Sunshine and shadow mark the history of the Church of Christ. It is one of the mysterious things that good men have been so imperfect.

1. *Redemption ends* when Christ comes. The passages which imply this are many. We select these: "Occupy till I come" (Luke xix. 13); "Gird up the loins of your mind, be sober, and hope to the end for the grace that is to be brought unto you at the revelation of Jesus Christ" (1 Pet. i. 13); "Go ye therefore, and teach all nations, baptizing them in the name of the Father, and of the Son, and of the Holy Ghost: teaching them to observe all things whatsoever I have commanded you: and lo, I am with you alway, even unto the *end of the* world" (Matt. xxviii. 19, 20); "For as

often as ye eat this bread, and drink this cup, ye do show the Lord's death *till he come.*" 1 Cor. xi. 26. Thus the second coming of Christ is the end of the means of grace and the end of the Spirit's striving with men.

2. The *righteous* and the *wicked* will be *raised* when Christ comes. " The hour is coming, in the which all that are in the graves shall hear his voice, and shall come forth; they that have done good, unto the resurrection of life; and they that have done evil, unto the resurrection of damnation." John v. 28, 29. However long or short the "hour" of the resurrection may be, it is during the passage of it that *all the dead arise.*

3. The *final judgment* takes place when Christ comes. The tares and wheat are to grow together till the harvest. Then the tares are burned and the wheat is preserved. Thus the destiny of the righteous and the wicked is settled at that time. In the twenty-fifth chapter of Matthew the good are ranged on the right hand and the bad on the left. The one class enter into eternal life, and the other class are consigned to eternal punishment. " We must *all* appear before the judgment-seat of Christ; that every one may receive the things done in his body, according to that he hath done, whether it be *good* or *bad*." 2 Cor. v. 10.

4. The heavens and the earth shall be *burned up* when Christ comes. "The day of the Lord will come as a thief in the night; in the which the

heavens shall pass away with a great noise, and the elements shall melt with fervent heat, the earth also and the works that are therein shall be burned up." 2 Pet. iii. 10.

The pious men of the Old Testament looked forward to the *first* coming of Christ, and the pious men of the New Testament look forward to the *second* coming of Christ. The first advent crowns and ends the Jewish dispensation, and the second advent crowns and ends the Christian dispensation. The *faith* of the early Christians, as it centred in the crucified Redeemer, soon became *hope* in the glorified Redeemer. Some of them had either seen him or they conversed with men who had, and so he was near to them. The union of the disciples with their Master was so close that their identity seemed lost in his wondrous personality. Their life was *hid* with Christ.

As we read over the New Testament it would seem as if the second advent were a kind of *universal motive*. It is fastened to every phase of Christian experience and every change of outward condition. "Be patient, brethren, unto the coming of the Lord" (James v. 7); "And this know, that if the good man of the house had known what hour the thief would come, he would have watched, and not have suffered his house to be broken through. Be ye therefore ready also: for the Son of man cometh at an hour when ye think not." Luke xii. 39, 40. Appeals, encouragements, exhortations and warnings are confined to the time that *precedes* the second advent. If men are to be fitted for heaven after our Lord has come, they will need a new Bible.

The second coming of Christ is evidently viewed as the climax of all good. Matters will then be settled, troubles banished, hopes realized. The distance between the first and second advent is not thought of: the one is brought near to the other. The mind is full of emotion, and through the medium of that emotion it darts ahead, only eager to behold "the glorious appearing of the great God, and our Saviour Jesus Christ." It is the nature of love to sweep away the boundaries of time and space, "hasting" to reach the adorable One in whom is found all its joy.

Van Oosterzee has this reasonable thought: "That our Lord constantly represents his future coming as very near at hand was the natural consequence of the prophetic mode of view, in which the difference of time and space is thrown into the background. It was also practically necessary, if the exhortation to watchfulness and labor was to receive its highest impressiveness from the relative nearness of a decisive future, to come when not expected." . . . "The exact fixing of the time was not, in the view of our Lord, the main thing, so much as the lively exhibition of the fact of his approaching manifestation. The repeated references to this fact stood directly connected with the consolation and sanctification of his disciples, at which from first to last he principally aimed."*

CHAPTER IV.

THE RESURRECTION OF THE DEAD.

The doctrine of the resurrection teaches that *man* as such is to exist as a complex being for ever. The human reason can give no information on this subject. The Bible alone reveals it. "As in Adam all die, even so in Christ shall all be made alive" (1 Cor. xv. 22); "There shall be a resurrection of the dead, both of the just and unjust" (Acts xxiv. 15); "I delivered unto you first of all that which I also received, how that Christ died for our sins according to the Scriptures: and that he was buried, and that he rose again the third day according to the Scriptures: and that he was seen of Cephas, then of the twelve: after that, he was seen of above five hundred brethren at once; of whom the greater part remain unto this present, but some are fallen asleep. After that, he was seen of James; then of all the apostles. And last of all he was seen of me also, as of one born out of due time." 1 Cor. xv. 3–7. If Christ has risen from the dead, that settles the matter. If there is no resurrection, Christianity is a fiction.

* *Biblical Theology of the New Testament*, pp. 78, 79.

I. Two Leading Objections.

1. It is affirmed by some persons that when a person dies he enters eternity with a *body*, and that that is the resurrection. This theory supposes that each man has two bodies—one of gross material, and the other finer. The fine body is next to the soul, and with that it enters the immortal state at death, needing no other for ever. This is the view of the Swedenborgians and some of the Spiritualists. There is no evidence, however, that such a spirit-body exists. Some of the ancient philosophers speculated in regard to the existence of such an airy kind of body. "They conceived this spirituous body to hang about the soul in this life as its anterior induement or vestment, which then sticks to it when that other gross earthly part of the body is, by death, put off as an outer garment." They even thought that there is "a third kind of body, of a higher rank than either of the former, peculiarly belonging to such souls after death as are cleansed from corporeal affections, lusts and passions, called by them a luciform, celestial and ethereal body." *

Even if we believe that the soul has a body in which it lives after death, what has that to do with the resurrection of the dead? It has nothing to do with it. The scriptural idea of the resurrection is not that of a soul going into eternity with a body which it always had. If such were the true idea, the resurrection is *past* to all who have died. The

* Cudworth's *Intellectual System*, vol. ii. pp. 222, 223.

Bible, however, speaks of the resurrection as *future:* it takes place at the end of the world. The point is also mentioned that the dead are to come out of their *graves.* But there is no grave to come out of if the spirit-body is the only one which the soul shall ever possess. The most dangerous thing, however, about this theory is, that it leads to the denial of Christ's resurrection, for if the body that dies is not raised again, then Christ is not risen.

2. The other objection is, that the bodies of the living have portions of matter which once belonged to the bodies of the dead; consequently, it is impossible for all the dead to be raised. This is the philosophical objection to the resurrection. It is not the abstract question whether God has *power* to raise the dead, but rather this, How can he do a thing that is physically impossible. As weakening the objection, we are not to understand that all parts of the body that dies are raised up. It is an admitted truth that "four-fifths of the bulk of most organisms is made up of formed matter. Only *one-fifth* is really alive." The Bible says plainly enough that "flesh and blood cannot inherit the kingdom of God." Our thought, then, is this: that amid all the changes of time God preserves the chief constituents of every body. Parts of bodies in the grave may enter into vegetation, and man may eat the food thus formed; yet God takes care of those elements which are needed for the future body. A person may eat a thousand pounds of

food in a year, yet at the end of the year be no heavier than he was at the beginning. It is easy, then, to understand how a living body may have particles which once belonged to a dead body, and yet all these particles in a short time be gone from it. In fact, every few years the body is composed of entirely new materials.

II. Nature of the Resurrection Body.

Persons assert that the *same body* which dies is the one that shall be raised again. It does not seem that these persons can mean what they say. The body that is suitable for this earth is certainly not suitable for heaven. Here we need food and drink, but these will not be needed in the other life. If the saints are to arise and meet the Lord in the air, and with him ascend to heaven, they must have different bodies from what they have at present.

1. The body will be *spiritual*. This does not mean that it will be a substance like the soul. The fact that it is a "body" shows that it is material. The language of Paul is, "There is a natural body, and there is a spiritual body." 1 Cor. xv. 44. The one is suited to the earthly life, and the other to the heavenly.

2. The future body will be *immortal*. "This corruptible must put on incorruption, and this mortal must put on immortality." 1 Cor. xv. 53. The implication here is, that there will be no principle of decay in that wondrous body.

3. The future body will be characterized by *great power*. Here the body is weak. Its strength has to be kept up by nourishment and rest. The incorruptible body will have no sense of weariness—simply power in action or power in repose. God will sustain it just as he sustains the soul. If the saints should be sent off to distant worlds on some great mission, the body will not be injured by any change.

4. The body will have a *splendid appearance*. "Christ shall change our vile body, that it may be fashioned like unto his glorious body." Phil. iii. 21. It will thus be exceedingly attractive and beautiful, shining with celestial radiance. It will be the fit habitation of a perfected soul, the fit temple of the Holy Spirit.

5. We infer that the glorified body will be *simple* in its construction. Our earthly body is intricate. The wonder is how it holds together for so many years. When we think of electricity and light, what powers they are in nature, and yet how simple, we catch the thought that the celestial body may be reduced to a few component parts. The more simple a machine is, the more likely it will be to keep in order. When we think of a body that is capable of living in any part of the universe, capable of great speed and fitted to endure for ever, we naturally suppose that both in its material and structure it must be simple.

6. The future body will have the *human form*.

When Moses and Elias appeared on the mount with Christ they were veritable men. Adam and Jesus had the human form. A great deal is to be attached to the fact that the Son of God assumed *our nature*. He will stand forth as the God-man for ever. The divine idea evidently is, that there shall always be a race of *men* who shall always point to the incarnate Redeemer as the one who saved them. Still, though the resurrection body will have the human form, I can understand how it may be modified at many points. Instead of five senses, there may be fifty. There are doubtless phases of mind and matter of which we know nothing. The future body may be so constituted that these phases will be discovered.

Touching the bodies of the wicked the Bible is silent. They may be deformed, bearing the marks of sin and uneasy with pain. A punitive element may thus be connected with them, making the body a kind of perdition. Even in this life there are bodies that are all unstrung. There is startling meaning in the passage, " Fear him which is able to destroy both soul and *body* in hell." Matt. x. 28. " In the present state we find that the mind has an immense power over the body, and, when diseased, often communicates disease to its sympathizing companion. I believe that in the future state the mind will have this power of conforming its outward frame to itself, incomparably more than here. We must never forget that in that world mind or character is to exert an all-powerful sway; and, accordingly, it is rational to believe that the corrupt and deformed mind which wants moral goodness, or a spirit of concord with God and with the universe, will create for itself, as its fit dwelling, a deformed body, which will also want concord or harmony with all things around it." *

CHAPTER V.

THE FINAL JUDGMENT.

THE persons to be judged at the final judgment are fallen men and fallen angels. It is true that judgments strike down men and nations in the present life, but these are different from the judgment of the great day. "All judgments in the world's history and by its means are merely partial, ambiguous and definitively decisive of nothing." The leading judgments seem to be *types* of the last judgment. The Saviour led the minds of men back to the time of Noah, and made them face that deluge which overwhelmed the world of the ungodly: "For as in the days that were before the flood they were eating and drinking, marrying and giving in marriage, until the day that Noah entered into the ark, and knew not until the flood came, and took them all away; so shall also the

* Dr. Channing, *Works*, vol. iv. p. 164.

coming of the Son of man be." Matt. xxiv. 38, 39. The apostle Peter calls attention to the same thought, using it to meet those scoffers who ask, "Where is the promise of his coming?" "For this they willingly are ignorant of, that by the word of God the heavens were of old, and the earth standing out of the water and in the water: whereby the world that then was, being overflowed with water, perished: but the heavens and the earth, which are now, by the same word are kept in store, reserved unto fire against the day of judgment and perdition of ungodly men." 2 Pet. iii. 5–7. The evils which fell upon Jerusalem are made also to symbolize the final judgment, for Christ passes from the one scene to the other as it were without a break: "Then shall appear the sign of the Son of man in heaven: and then shall all the tribes of the earth mourn, and they shall see the Son of man coming in the clouds of heaven with power and great glory. And he shall send his angels with a great sound of a trumpet, and they shall gather together his elect from the four winds, from one end of heaven to the other." Matt. xxiv. 30, 31. By looking at earthly judgments in this way we behold preludes of the day of doom, as if heralds were standing at these crises of history and were sounding forth in clear notes, THE FINAL JUDGMENT IS CERTAIN.

The soul of man also points to a future judgment. Guilt sees retribution ahead, thus harmonizing with Scripture when it speaks of "a certain fearful looking-for of judgment and fiery indignation." "He who 'sees the end from the beginning' has imparted to man a subordinate prescience of the same comprehensive kind, has sketched on his mind an outline of the great system of providence, and filled him with presentiments of the principal events which are to attend the development of that system. The consequence is, that wherever the Bible comes it finds our nature preconfigured to many of its truths, waiting for an interpreter, and ready to respond to the truth of many a prediction as a prophecy or an anticipation with which it had long been familiar in thought." *

1. Passages which prove a future judgment. "The angels which kept not their first estate, but left their own habitation, he hath reserved in everlasting chains under darkness unto the judgment of the great day" (Jude 6); "When the Son of man shall come in his glory, and all the holy angels with him, then shall he sit upon the throne of his glory: and before him shall be gathered all nations: and he shall separate them one from another, as a shepherd divideth his sheep from the goats: and he shall set the sheep on his right hand, but the goats on the left" (Matt. xxv. 31–34); "And I saw the dead, small and great, stand before God; and the books were opened: and another

* Dr. Harris, *The Great Teacher*, p. 263.

book was opened which is the book of life: and the dead were judged out of those things which were written in the books, according to their works." Rev. xx. 12. These passages show that the judgment is to be at the end of the world, at the time Christ comes with his angels—when the human race and the fallen angels are convened before him.

2. Christ is the Judge. We read of "the judgment-seat of Christ," and that "God hath committed all judgment to the Son." It is suitable that the divine-human Redeemer should be the Judge of fallen angels, inasmuch as they established and extended the kingdom of evil upon this earth —suitable that he should be the Judge of fallen men, inasmuch as they lived under a remedial system. He is now to bring out in a public manner how the race acted with reference to a way of salvation. While man's relation to the divine law will be made apparent, his relation to the divine remedy will be the most conspicuous. Whether each one is penitent or impenitent, believing or unbelieving, will settle the matter for ever. With the Saviour and the sinner face to face, the elements of the trial will be made to stand out and the whole be greatly simplified. The fact, also, that Christ is the Judge shows that he must be divine, for no creature, however high, is sufficient for such a work.

3. As it respects the manner of the judgment

and the time it will occupy, the Bible does not fully inform us. That each person will go through a lengthened examination is not likely. There will be such a vivid consciousness at that time that the judgment process can go forward with rapidity. That the trial will occupy scores or hundreds of years seems out of the question. The electric movement of minds on the one hand, and the sweep of divinity on the other, will no doubt bring the matter to a close in a short time. The future body may have such adaptation to the soul that the entire history of that soul may appear as in panoramic vision. Each man thus left to himself, conscience may pronounce sentence with great truthfulness. The sense of justice will be so clear that every knee shall bow and every tongue confess to the equity of Christ's decision.

4. The question is frequently asked, "If souls are judged after death, why is it necessary to have a public judgment for all mankind?" It is not easy to answer this question. Still, one or two thoughts may be suggested.

We should try and realize that truth and justice are not merely related to individual souls, but that they have an extensive bearing on the entire government of God. There are various orders of intelligent beings in the divine system besides fallen men and fallen angels, and the dealings of God with reference to the sinful are to affect those who have never sinned. Then, too, the facts that the human race have finished their career upon earth; that the redemptive period is ended; that the world is to be burned up and a new chapter of providence to begin; that the wicked are to mingle no more with the good, but are to work out their mysterious destiny by themselves,—these striking realities may make a public judgment to be necessary. It should be considered also that a man's influence does not stop at the moment of death; it goes from soul to soul for generations, even down to the end of time, so that a judgment at the end of human history may be the only way in which character can receive its rights.

No doubt persons are perplexed about this subject, because they believe that there is no other punishment than remorse of conscience. If remorse of conscience is all, then the entire scheme of outward jurisprudence is set aside. If it were the rule of nations that crime could be punished only by remorse, there would be no statute law, no court to try men, no officers of justice, no prisons. If this is the way to view the divine government, then there is no accountability to God—each man is accountable simply to himself; there is no relation to an outward law—each man is supreme law; there is no outward punishment to fear—each man punishes himself. It is not "Vengeance is mine; I will repay, saith the *Lord;*" but, Vengeance is mine; I will repay, saith the *conscience.* Carry out this theory, and of course there is no public judgment. A positive moral government is swept away by it entirely. Even the atonement is made impossible by it, because the atonement relates to an outward law and penalty—relates to God as Judge and Ruler. Thus the necessity of a public judgment arises from the fact that man has broken an objective law, is exposed to an objective punishment, and has had a day of grace which was the result of an objective atonement.

CHAPTER VI.

THE FUTURE PUNISHMENT OF THE WICKED.

PUNISHMENT is *not* of the nature of *discipline*. That a man to avoid pain will abstain from certain evils is a fact; and yet pain never makes a man love holiness and hate sin. The Bible language touching divine punishment is very different from the language which expresses fatherly discipline. Note these passages: "The same shall drink of the wine of the wrath of God, which is poured out without mixture into the cup of his indignation; and he shall be tormented with fire and brimstone in the presence of the holy angels, and in the presence of the Lamb" (Rev. xiv. 10); "If I whet my glittering sword, and mine hand take hold on judgment; I will render vengeance to mine enemies, and will reward them that hate me" (Deut. xxxii. 41); "If any man love not the Lord Jesus

Christ, let him be Anathema Maranatha." 1 Cor. xvi. 22. The idea of discipline does not appear in these verses. See the difference in the following passages: "Blessed is the man whom thou chastenest, O Lord, and teachest him out of thy law; that thou mayest give him rest from the days of adversity, until the pit be digged for the wicked" (Ps. xciv. 12, 13); "My son, despise not the chastening of the Lord; neither be weary of his correction: for whom the Lord loveth he correcteth; even as a father the son in whom he delighteth" (Prov. iii. 11, 12); "Our light affliction, which is but for a moment, worketh for us a far more exceeding and eternal weight of glory." 2 Cor. iv. 17. Thus Love chastens the righteous, while Justice punishes the wicked.

The true idea of punishment can be gained only from the true idea of sin. Sin has the quality of demerit, and a man is punished because he is guilty —punished whether he becomes better or worse. If penal suffering has the power to change malice into love, it is a *blessing* and not a curse.

Future punishment is *not annihilation*. Because men *die*, that is no evidence that they are annihilated. The *body* only is dead; the soul lives. That is the way that such language has generally been understood. The fact that "the Lord is the God of Abraham, and the God of Isaac, and the God of Jacob" is proof, according to Christ, that "he is not a God of the dead, but of the *living*." Luke

xx. 37, 38. These men were dead as to their bodies, but they were living as to their souls. Then the unconverted are spoken of as "dead," and yet they live an intense life. "She that liveth in pleasure is *dead* while she *liveth*." 1 Tim. v. 6.

The words "destroy," "devour," "consume," are quoted as conveying the idea of annihilation. The Bible is a strange book if its language is to be understood in that way. We meet with such statements as these: "The destruction of the poor is their poverty" (Prov. x. 15); "My people are destroyed for lack of knowledge" (Hos. iv. 6); "O Israel, thou hast destroyed thyself." Hos. xiii. 9. How plain it is that these classes were not actually destroyed! Then we read of those who "*bite* and *devour* one another" (Gal. v. 15), as if the individuals were eaten up, when, as matter of fact, they simply manifested a bitter spirit. David says, "My bones are *consumed*;" "I am consumed by the blow of thine hand" (Ps. xxxix. 10), and yet he was living at that very time. Jacob, expressing the hardness of his lot, says: "In the day the drought consumed me, and the frost by night." Gen. xxxi. 40. Such language has nothing to do with utter extinction of being. "A man is broken down with sorrow, crushed with calamity, lacerated with grief, rent with anguish, melted with emotion, when every faculty of mind and body is sound and whole. He is prostrated with fear, is irretrievably fallen, is ruined—not in body, but in soul—when yet the substance and all the powers of his soul remain untouched. He is eaten up by avarice, racked with anxiety, devoured by ambition, consumed with lust, sunk in vice, drowned in sorrow, burned up with fierce and evil passions, and that, too, when his being and all its essential functions are so far from extinct that they are in a state of the most intense activity."*

Endless punishment is *endless suffering*. To be out of existence is to suffer nothing. When a man is hung we do not call that everlasting punishment. If a village is burned to ashes, that is not everlasting fire. The unfaithful servant is represented as *cut asunder*, and yet *after* that he is in the place where "there is *weeping* and *gnashing* of teeth." The finally impenitent "have *no rest* day nor night;" "the smoke of their *torment* ascendeth up for ever and ever." Much of the language which relates to the punishment of the wicked and the blessedness of the righteous is figurative, and the mistake is in thinking that it is literal. Christ says that "everlasting fire" was prepared for the devil and his angels, and yet the devil and his angels are *spirits*, and so cannot be affected by fire. If to sink into nothingness is the punishment due to sin, then the greatest sinner and the least are punished alike. Annihilation is simply a theory. It is an attempt to soften the severity of the divine administration.

* Bartlett, *Life and Death Eternal*, p. 27.

Persons say that endless punishment is unreasonable. No importance can be attached to a statement of this kind, because the subject is beyond the reach of the human understanding. There is not a single leading doctrine of Christianity but has been pronounced unreasonable. The incarnation of the Son of God, the Christian atonement, total depravity, regeneration by the Spirit, justification by faith, the resurrection of the dead, have all been considered unreasonable. No thoughtful person, then, will allow himself to be governed by the mere assertions of sinful and shortsighted men. Even if I admit that there is something strange about endless punishment, yet when I look at other phases of creaturely existence I find things that are equally perplexing. It is certain that thousands of human beings have been destroyed by fire and angry seas, by earthquakes and volcanic eruptions, by famine and plague, and yet God did not intervene. He heard the cries of suffering people as life wore out in agony, but he did not save them. Take the collective sin and pain that have devoured mankind since the beginning of time, and the picture is fearful. It is evident that there is severity with God as well as goodness. How strange that a Being of infinite power, wisdom and love should have selected a system with evil in it! Taking my reason as guide, I should say that he would have selected a system in which all the persons would be holy and happy. He has not done, however, what to me seems the best. The same argument, then, which affirms that sin must end affirms that sin must not begin; for to the human reason the one seems to clash as much with the divine character as the other. The argument, therefore, falls to pieces and cannot be used. If men will use it, they should see that its logical outcome is atheism. The atheist says that sin and suffering are evidences that there is no God, because if there were such a Being he never would permit such evils to afflict the race.

Our safety, then, is to leave human opinion and go to divine revelation. The question being too far-reaching for us to settle, we allow God to settle it for us. Faith takes the place of reason, inasmuch as it can do no better, and by the very act proves itself to be reasonable. Persons, however, insist that the word translated "everlasting" in the Bible has a limited meaning. Yes; all limitless words have a limited meaning at times, as when I say, "The eternal stars," "the everlasting mountains," "the infinite sea." Scripture falls in with this style when it speaks of the land of Canaan as an "everlasting possession," with its "everlasting statute" and "everlasting priesthood." That the word has the sense of *age* also is true. We read of "the cares of this age," "the wisdom of this age" and "the end of this age," the word "world" being used in our translation instead of "age." If now we say that the Greek word rendered "everlasting" has simply the meaning of age-long, we stultify ourselves. Let us apply it to *heaven* and see how it will work:

"He that believeth on the Son hath everlasting life" (John iii. 36); shall we say, "Hath age-long life"? "Our light affliction, which is but for a moment, worketh for us a far more exceeding and eternal weight of glory" (2 Cor. iv. 17); shall we say, "Age-long weight of glory"? "That they may also obtain the salvation which is in Christ Jesus with eternal glory" (2 Tim. ii. 10); "With age-long glory"? "This is the true God, and eternal life" (1 John v. 20); "Age-long life"? "Looking for the mercy of our Lord Jesus Christ unto eternal life" (Jude 21); "Unto age-long life"? Thus the blessedness of heaven is to continue simply for an age. In order to cut short the miseries of the lost we must cut short the joys of the saved. If the same method is applied to *God*, he is equally limited, and by that very limitation is annihilated.

There is no reason why the duration of punishment should be any shorter than the duration of reward. The language is clear enough: "These shall go away into everlasting punishment: but the righteous into life eternal." Matt. xxv. 46. Here the same word is used in both cases. If I must limit the pain, I must limit the peace; so the time will come when the righteous shall be lost and the wicked shall be saved. Then, too, if the punishment of ungodly men must end, we must go a step farther, and say, with Origen, that the punishment of the fallen angels must end. Having gone as far as this, we may as well begin to pray for lost souls and these lost spirits that their punitive training may speedily fit them for heaven. Scripture language, however, conveys the idea that the destiny of the good and the bad is *fixed* and *final*. He that is unjust is to be unjust still, and he that is righteous is to be righteous still. Let sin once take hold of a soul, and that soul is doomed. We cannot conceive of a time when it will retire from the creaturely spirit. Simply give sin a place in the universe, and from its nature it is eternal. No one can point to a single fallen being who has restored himself to holiness. Length of time, instead of weakening sin, only strengthens it. The antediluvians, whose age was almost a thousand years, became worse and worse. It is an act of mercy that God has shortened the life of man.

The drift of Bible-teaching is in the direction of endless punishment. As if to arrest our attention and impress us most solemnly, the compassionate Redeemer is the one who speaks more frequently of the woes of hereafter than any other person in Scripture. Theodore Parker was sufficiently truthful to say: "I believe that Jesus Christ taught eternal torments." He was daring enough, however, to add, "I do not accept it on his authority." Dr. Davidson speaks in the same way. "If a specific sense be attached to words," he remarks, "never-ending misery is enunciated. On the presumption that one doctrine is taught, it is the eternity of hell-torments. Bad exegesis may attempt to banish it from the New-Testament Scriptures, but it is still there; and expositors who wish to get rid of it, as Canon Farrar does, injure the cause they have in view by misinterpretation." Having admitted that the Bible teaches the doctrine, he now lets us know that he does not believe it. "If a provision be not made in revelation," he says, "for a change of moral character after death, it is made in *reason*. Philosophical considerations must not be set aside even by Scripture."

It is a significant fact that the Church of God, with a few exceptions, has held to the belief that the wicked shall be punished for ever. It is no less significant that all skeptics deny the eternity of punishment. Is it likely that men who reject the Bible are right in their denial of endless punishment, while men who receive the Bible are wrong in their believing it? Certainly, the probabilities are that the truth lies with the collective body of Christians, and not with the collective body of skeptics.

When Noah proclaimed that God would destroy the world of the ungodly with a flood, no doubt they affirmed that such a thing would be unreasonable and unjust, and that it never could take place. They were all swept away, however, without mercy. So will it be with the finally impenitent in the future state. That sin is against an infinite Being shows that punishment must be exceedingly great. If God had to become man, and as man suffer and die in order to make atonement, sin must be a tremendous evil. A divine atonement and endless punishment stand or fall together. If we strike down the one, we strike down the other. It is the nature of one to illustrate and measure the other.

There is even a sin mentioned in Scripture which places those who commit it beyond all hope. " He that shall blaspheme against the Holy Ghost hath never forgiveness, but is in danger of eternal damnation." Mark iii. 29. Or rendered thus : " Hath never forgiveness, but is guilty of an eternal sin." He is subject to eternal sin, and so is lost for ever. It is said of Judas, " It had been good for that man if he had not been born." Matt. xxvi. 24. If the betrayer of Christ would ultimately be saved, it would not seem proper to say of him that it would have been better if he had not been born. An eternity of joy would far outweigh a few years of pain. The only fair inference, then, is that Judas is hopelessly lost.

There are persons who believe in the supremacy of free will—believe that they can resist any influence which God might bring to bear upon them with reference to their salvation. Very well. Let this be as these persons say. They turn not from evil ; they will not accept of mercy : they are determined to have their own way. How can it be wrong to leave such individuals to themselves? What else can be done with them, since their will is stronger than divine grace? It is not in point to speak of God as unjust in punishing them. They take the matter in their own hand and accept the consequences of their manner of life. If they were really injured by outside pressure, they might be objects of pity, but since they freely prefer their own course, that is the end of it. Their character never changes, because they want no change. Their punishment is endless, because by a fixed choice they have adopted sin with all its results. If we tell them that separation from God is one part of eternal punishment, they answer that they have no desire to be near to God. If we say that they will be banished from the society of the good in heaven, they reply that that to them is no evil. They prefer to mingle with their own kind, gratifying their own tastes as they think proper. Thus, accepting their situation with all its evils, they are left and lost.

CHAPTER VII.

THE FUTURE REWARDS OF THE RIGHTEOUS.

"Heaven" is a notable word. It points to a holy place, and not merely to a holy state. The place is viewed as above us. It contains all excellencies, as if it were the ideal realm of the universe. The angels make their home there. Christ came from heaven to this earth to work out salvation for lost men, and when the work was finished he went back again to heaven. To show the high dignity of the place, God is spoken of as "the Lord of heaven," "the King of heaven" and as "our Father which art in heaven." All interests appear to centre there, as if heaven were the capital of the universe, creatures going to it and coming from it on some exalted mission. The divine glories are evidently manifested there with such splendor and fullness as are found nowhere else, and the worship which ascends there to God is remarkable for its purity, intelligence and compass.

It is to this world of light that the saints go to obtain the reward promised them. There is "an inheritance incorruptible, and undefiled, and that fadeth not away, reserved in heaven for you" (1 Pet. i. 4); "Rejoice, and be exceeding glad: for great is your reward in heaven." Matt. v. 12. This thought of heaven has grasped all Christian souls. It gives color to their thinking, forms their stay in hours of darkness, presses them forward in times of depression. Heaven partakes of the final and ultimate. The mind rests in it as if it were the symbol of God, its beauty being fairer than all fair things, and the day which marks it off being nothing less than the day of the Lord. Even the wicked dream of it, sighing in exile because they have lost it; the thought of it sharpening their pain, the glory of it deepening their night.

Heaven has about it an *organic* idea. The people who live there form a society. They have a single corporate life. Hence we see heaven as a "city," a "country," a "kingdom." "We feel that we are taken up into a scheme of things which is in conflict with the present, and which cannot realize itself here. Therefore our final teaching is by prophecy, which shows us, not how we are personally saved and victorious, but how the battle goes upon the whole, and which issues in the appearance of a holy city in which redemption reaches its end and the Redeemer finds his joy; in which human tendencies are realized and divine promises fulfilled; in which the ideal has become the actual, and man is perfected in the presence and glory of God."*

There is a principle which belongs to the very nature of moral government—namely, this: that "whatsoever a man soweth, that shall he also reap." Gal. vi. 7. Good and evil work out for ever by a law of their own; and by that law the one ends in joy and the other in misery. This is simply a fact seen in thousands of instances, and can admit of no dispute. The point is to realize it, and to feel that this constitution of nature cannot be changed. The moral system will work out inexorably, irrespective of all wishes to the con-

* Bernard, *Progress of Doct. in New Test.*, p. 225.

trary. Sin never will succeed; holiness never will fail. "Say ye to the righteous, that it shall be well with him: for they shall eat the fruit of their doings. Woe unto the wicked! it shall be ill with him: for the reward of his hands shall be given him." Isa. iii. 10, 11.

1. The rewards of heaven are a matter of *grace.* "The gift of God is eternal life through Jesus Christ our Lord." Rom. vi. 23. That the holiest men are imperfect shows that they cannot merit heaven. The law demands perfect obedience every moment. Even if one should reach perfection, he cannot make up for the sins of the past. There are no works of supererogation, and repentance cannot satisfy the law. He who sheds blood is put to death, whether he repents or not. If a man turns from sin, it is the grace of God which enables him to turn. If he believes in Christ, and by that means is saved, the merit is not in the faith, but in the Saviour. "By grace are ye saved through faith; and that not of yourselves: it is the gift of God." Eph. ii. 8. Actions may be performed which have in them an element of holiness, yet without the Divine Spirit they never would be performed; so that, taking the Christian life in its totality, there is no such thing as salvation by works. Even the reward of sinless beings is partly a gift. The holiness with them is not absolute. They were created with a pure disposition and with a will that was inclined to obedience.

They had the Spirit to influence them, and thus they are debtors to God. "All finite holiness," says Professor Shedd, "be it in man or angel, is only *relatively* meritorious, because it is the result of God's working in man or angel to will and to do."*

Even in regard to the natural happiness of creatures, God might have made it less without doing them any injury. All the happiness, beyond a small degree, is to be viewed as the result of sovereignty, and not as the result of justice. Although the Divine Being might not consistently form an organism for the express purpose of producing pain, he might form an organism that would average ten degrees of pleasure instead of one hundred. Our delight in form and color, in variety and novelty, might be greatly lessened if God had so desired; and even the gift of music, which adds so much to the enjoyment of mankind, might have been withheld altogether without any injustice. *Sin is man's own.* The will is *self*-moved when it goes into evil, and so the punishment is meted out according to strict justice. Whatever the degree of wickedness, the punishment will be proportioned to that degree. "That servant, which knew his lord's will, and prepared not himself, neither did according to his will, shall be beaten with many stripes. But he that knew not, and did commit things worthy of stripes, shall be beaten with few stripes." Luke xii. 47, 48. All of the finally and

* *Hist. of Christian Doct.*, vol. ii. p. 54.

incorrigibly impenitent will suffer for ever, but the suffering will vary as to intensity.

2. Though heavenly rewards are of grace, they are graded according to *faithfulness*. The man whose pound gained five pounds was placed over *five cities*, while the other was placed over *ten cities* because his pound had increased to ten. The penitent robber will not have a reward equal to that of the apostle Paul. The Bible speaks of those who are "saved so as by fire," of those who have an "abundant entrance" into the heavenly kingdom, and of those who will "shine as the stars for ever and ever." Every converted man will reach heaven, and every vessel will be filled at the fountain of life; but the vessels will differ in size and value. There will thus be different ranks of glorified men. Some will teach, and some will be taught. There will be kingly minds who will travel far and long, attending to great interests in the system of God, while others will work in lower spheres with faithfulness and love. Each saved immortal will be holy and happy, but the volume of holiness and happiness will differ.

3. Though the rewards of heaven are of grace, and are graded according to faithfulness, they are all *greatly beyond proportion* to man's doings. It is not that two acts of love are followed by two blessings of the same weight and worth as the love. The blessings are manifold, and quite high as to their wealth. The servant that was faithful

over a *few* things is made ruler over *many* things. No doubt God has a rule in the bestowment of rewards. But just what that rule is we cannot say. We can only affirm that the divine rewards are exceedingly munificent. When we think of the deficiencies of the noblest men, and then see the eternal weight of glory that shall come to them, we are surprised.

The beatific vision of God will be the culminating reward of the saved. According to the texture of each soul, and the amount of the divine which is in it, so will be its nearness to the Deity. "God will be so known by us," says Augustine, "and shall be so much before us, that we shall see him by the spirit in ourselves, in one another, in himself, in the new heavens and the new earth, in every created thing which shall then exist; and also by the body we shall see him in every body which the keen vision of the eye of the spiritual body shall reach." . . . "How great shall be that felicity which shall be tainted with no evil, which shall lack no good, and which shall afford leisure for the praises of God, who shall be all in all! For I know not what other employment there can be where no lassitude shall slacken activity nor any want stimulate to labor." . . . "God shall be the end of our desires, who shall be seen without end, loved without cloy, praised without weariness."* When we try to imagine how the soul

* *City of God*, vol. ii. pp. 540, 541.

will increase in knowledge, goodness and blessedness for ever, we are simply confused by excellencies that are limitless.

Wonderful life! May we reach it at the end of our day! We shall think of it during the quick beat of the moments, hastening our steps that we may come to it in peace. We long for the country that we have never seen. As the sun shines across some great river at the evening time, forming a beautiful bridge of light from shore to shore, as if it were the royal path where angels walk at the close of the day, so the sun of eternity sends its radiance across the river of death, forming a golden highway for souls to pass over to their home in heaven. When we shall reach the Land of God we shall know no evil thing. With easy step we shall travel along our way. Seraphs and saints shall be our friends. We shall ascend the heights of the Lord. God shall be to us all in all. Glorious Being, help us! We wander as yet through clouds; shine upon us! When the morning comes we shall be well. Till then we shall trust and toil. Our life shall be a prayer until home is reached. We shall enter the city-gates with songs and joy.

"Blessing, and honor, and glory, and power, be unto him that sitteth upon the throne, and unto the Lamb for ever and ever!"

INDEX.

ABILITY, gracious, 144.
Ability, natural, 84.
Ackermann, Dr., 101.
Addison, Joseph, on immortality of the soul, 92.
Advent, Second, 207.
Agnosticism, 15.
Anderson, Christopher, on family prayer, 174.
Angels, creation of, 46; nature of, 46.
Angels, fallen, 48.
Annihilation, 192, 225.
Argyll, duke of, on evolution, 59.
Assurance of faith and hope, 161.
Atonement, necessity of, on part of man, 115; on part of God, 116; atonement vicarious, 117; Christ a redemptive person, 117; the atonement a satisfaction to justice, 118; infinite value of, 119; sufferings of Christ penal, 119; extent of atonement, 121; intercession of Christ, 122.
Augustine on original sin, 71; on beatific vision, 240.

BACON, LORD, on atheism, 20; on Christ as Mediator, 125.
Baptismal regeneration, 149.
Bartlett, Samuel, on the theory of annihilation, 227.
Beet, Joseph, 142.
Bernard, Joseph, 236.

CALDERWOOD, DR., on miracles, 52.

Calvin, John, on original sin, 71; on Christ as Mediator, 125.
Canons of Dort, 186.
Channing, Dr., 217.
Charnock, Stephen, on the atonement, 118.
Christ, divinity of, 105; no change in divine nature by the incarnation, 110; how Christ could be tempted, 112; second coming of, 206.
Cobb, Rev. William, on meaning of *ruah* and *nephesh*, 194.
Common grace, 138.
Comte, 128.
Conscience, 83.
Cowles, Dr., 195.
Covenants, 113.
Creation, days of, 42; double work on third and sixth days, 45.
Creeds of Christendom, 186, 196.
Cudworth on the First God, 13; on the spirit body, 213.

DANA, PROF., on the creation, 46.
Darwin, 59.
Davidson, Dr., 231.
Dawson, Dr., 59, 66.
Decrees of God, 36; decree and foreknowledge, 37; decree of God and sin, 40; mystery of the divine decrees, 147.
Delitzsch, Franz, 103.
Depravity, total, 80.
Dorner, Dr., 32, 105, 125.
Duff, Alexander, 145.

EARTH, the, antiquity of, 43.
Edwards, President, 168.
Efficacious grace, 152.
Election, all men not treated alike, 140; all men not good, 141; meaning of election, 142; idea of sufficient grace examined, 144; as man is totally depraved, God must take the first step, 145; if grace not stronger than depravity, all will be lost, 145.
Evil, origin and mystery of, 40, 74.

FAITH and reason, 155.
Faith, saving, what it is not, 156; what it is, 157; results of saving faith, 158.
Fall of man, how it took place and in what it consists, 69; relation of Adam to the race, 70; meaning of original sin, 71; evidence of original sin, 72; theories of the origin of sin, 73.
Flint implements, 63.
Foreknowledge of God, 37.
Foster, John, on prayer, 169.
Free agency of man, what it implies, 83; what it is, 86; relation of motives to the will, 87; cause of volition, 88; power of contrary choice, 89.
Future rewards, heaven the place of, 235; are of grace, 237; yet proportioned to faithfulness, 239; the rewards exceedingly great, 239.

GEOLOGY, 43, 59.
God, the universe a proof of his existence, 14; design points to a Designer, 16; human mind points to the divine mind, 18.
God, attributes of: eternity, 21; immutability, 22; omnipresence, 23; omnipotence, 23; omniscience, 24; wisdom, 25; self-determining power, 25; holiness, 26; justice, 27; love, 27; truth, 28.

God, ultimate end of, 35.
Golden Age, 204.

HARRIS, DR., 220.
Heaven, the good there after death, 194; the place of reward, 234.
Herodotus, 114.
Hodge, Archibald, 39.
Hodge, Charles, 34, 96, 154.
Holy Spirit, his personality, 132; divinity, 133; the procession of, 134; how his work is distinguished from that of the other divine Persons, 135; his relation to the man Christ Jesus, 136; inspires the Scripture-writers, 137; bestows unusual gifts, 138; applies the divine remedy to souls, 139.
Holy Spirit, sin against the, 79.
Howe, John, on sin as idolatry, 78.
Humanity, true idea of, from the Bible, 202.

IMAGE OF GOD, in what it consists, 67.
Immortality of the soul, proofs of, from reason, 90; from Scripture, 94.
Incarnation of Christ, 104.
Infants saved, 71, 144.
Intercession of Christ, 122.
Irish Articles of Religion, 196.
Judgment, last, 218.
Justification by faith, 158.

LAKE-DWELLINGS, 64.
Luthardt, Dr., 101.

MAN, origin and antiquity of, 58, 62.
Man, innocence and fall of, 67, 70.
Martensen, Dr., 93, 199.
Mediatorship of Christ, before redemption, 124; during redemption, 126; after redemption, 129.
Millennium, 198.
Miller, Rev. William, 199.

Miracles, 52.
Moral inability, 85.
Motive, what it is, 87.
Mulford, Dr., on the personality of God, 18.
Müller, Julius, on the unpardonable sin, 80.
Müller, Max, on the idea of humanity, 202.

NATURAL ABILITY, 84.
Neander, 125.
Need of redemption, as seen in the consciousness of loss, 98; unrest, 99; ideals not realized, 100; despair, 101.
Nitzsch, Dr., on Christ as Mediator, 125.

OWEN, JOHN, on the work of the Spirit, 136; on regeneration, 153.

PARKER, DR., 140.
Parker, Theodore, 231.
Perseverance of saints, 184.
Plan of God, 36.
Pope, Dr., 75, 153, 190.
Pottery in mud of River Nile, 62.
Power of contrary choice, 89.
Prayer, does not violate natural law, 168; nature of, 170; parts of prayer, 171; kinds of prayer, 173; prevailing prayer, 175.
Pressensé, Edmond de, 104.
Procter, Richard, 17.
Providence of God, definition of, 50; theory that God acts directly, 51; theory that God acts through second causes, 51; universal and special providence, 52; miracles, 53; providence by means of the fortuities of life, 54; providence does not destroy freedom, 55; God gives power, but does not prompt man to use that power to sin, 56; providential judgments, 56.
Punishment, future, not discipline, 224; not annihilation, 225; duration of punishment cannot be settled by reason, 228; limited meaning of everlasting, not true when applied to heaven, 230; endless punishment the doctrine of the Church in all ages, 232; what shall be done with those who will not be saved? 233.

RAYMOND, PROF., on regeneration, 153.
Regeneration, what it is not, 149; what it is, 151; Author of, 153.
Repentance, what it is not, 163; what it is, 164; reasons for, 166; evidence of, 167.
Resurrection, proofs of, 212; objections to, 213; the resurrection body, 215; bodies of the wicked, 217.

SANCTIFICATION, meaning of, 176; carried forward by the Spirit, 177; means of sanctification, 178; reached through conflict, 179; also by direct efforts, 181; is sinlessness attainable in this life? 182.
Schaff, Dr., 186, 196.
Second causes, God works through them in nature, 51, 126; in sanctification, 178.
Second coming of Christ, time of, not known, 207; present decline in religion not certain evidence that the time is near, 208; redemption ends when Christ comes, 208; dead are raised, 209; men judged, 209: earth burned up, 209; second advent a kind of universal motive, 210.
Shedd, Dr., 119, 203, 238.
Sin, a state of mind, 75; nature of sin, 77; entire sinfulness, 80.
Smith, Prof. H. B., on value of theology, 5; on creation, 15; on original sin, 70; on Christ

as the centre, 128; on election, 145.

Son of man, significance of the phrase, 107.

Soul, after death, does not sleep, 191; is not material, and so not out of existence after death, 192; soul of the righteous in blessedness, 194; of the wicked in misery, 196; no probation after death, 197.

Species, the higher, not evolved from lower, 59, 66.

Spencer, Herbert, 16.

Strauss, Dr., 111.

TAYLOR, ISAAC, on the fortuities of life, 54.

Triune God, not an impossible thing, 29; scriptural proof of the Trinity, 31; explanation of the doctrine, 33; the doctrine practical, 35.

Tulloch, Dr., on order as proving mind, 16.

VAN OOSTERZEE, DR., on the second advent, 211.

Vogt, C., 193.

WESTMINSTER CONFESSION, 143, 196.

Wiggers, Dr., 71.

Will, is it self-determining? 88.

Witness of the Spirit, 160.

THE END.

www.ingramcontent.com/pod-product-compliance
Lightning Source LLC
Chambersburg PA
CBHW020759230426